CHILD PRISONER

Child Prisoner

in American
Concentration Camps

By

Mako Nakagawa

Illustrations by

Mits Katayama

NewSage Press
Oregon

NewSage Press
PO Box 607
Troutdale, OR 97060

www.newsagepress.com
info@newsagepress.com

Cover & Book Design by Sherry Wachter

First Edition 2019

Distributed in the United States by Publishers Group West (PGW) / Ingram

Library of Congress Cataloging-in-Publication Data is available.

DEDICATION

To Mama and Papa,
my "Yaya" and "Papu"

–MAKO NAKAGAWA

To my dear granddaughter Sara,
with lots of love from Bumpa

–MITS KATAYAMA

"Let the legacy of the WW II imprisonment of Japanese Americans be that it never happens again to any group of people."

−A COMMON CRY
FROM ALL CORNERS OF THE
JAPANESE AMERICAN COMMUNITIES

CONTENTS

$\mathcal{P}$ROLOGUE

When I was a child, I was incarcerated in American concentration camps. I was a prisoner. I was not imprisoned in an "assembly center," a "relocation camp," or an "internment camp," I was forced into a concentration camp with my mother and three sisters when I was five years old. I was not "evacuated" as someone might be from a hurricane. We had to leave our home by a government order and armed guards herded us into concentration camps.

Words are important. Being honest about what happened has taken a long time.

As a child, my fantasy world of childhood stories abruptly came to an end. The Japanese fairy tale character Issunboshi, the one-inch boy with a needle for a sword, turned into a six-foot American soldier with a rifle. The Queen of Hearts in her castle was replaced by guards in towers with searchlights. Instead of a cottage with a white picket fence, I lived in barracks surrounded by barbed-wire fences. Yet, inside this harsh, brutal world, my parents protected me and my sisters as much as possible, and with all their hearts.

–MAKO NAKAGAWA
JUNE 2018

CHILD PRISONER

CHAPTER 1

BIRTHDAY CAKE & THE FBI

February 21, 1942 was set to be a pleasant day for the Takahashi family. It was my eldest sister's birthday. Kazu said her eleventh birthday was a very special birthday, but the second oldest sister, Nobu, piped up with "she says that every year...."

Kazu ignored her younger sister's comment. She was two years older than her sister Nobu, at least until Nobu turned ten on her birthday in July. Excited, Kazu had difficulty falling asleep, anticipating her birthday. My fifth birthday had been twenty days earlier, and it was certainly a memorable day for me. I had hoped we would celebrate Kazu's birthday with just as much fun. For certain, Mama would make some of Kazu's favorite dishes for dinner and we would have birthday cake for dessert. None of us anticipated the terrible day that would unfold—the day our world was turned upside down.

That fateful morning, all the ingredients to make Kazu's birthday cake sat on the kitchen counter. Mama had put them out the night before in preparation to bake Kazu's cake first thing in the morning. But in the pre-dawn hours while my family slept, a change in the United States had already begun to unfold—a change that would make this day life-altering for our family and for tens-of-thousands of other people of Japanese descent living in America.

Two days earlier, President Franklin Delano Roosevelt had signed Executive Order 9066. This presidential order gave the U.S. military the authority to forcibly remove and incarcerate anyone they determined to be a threat to the security of the nation, regardless of whether or not they were U.S. citizens. The government used this order to forcibly remove people of Japanese descent living in the western United States.

However, even before Executive Order 9066 was signed on February 19, 1942, the U.S. government had previously been investigating various Japanese, German, and Italian immigrants as potential threats to the security of the United States. On Dec. 7, 1941, the day Pearl Harbor was bombed, the FBI and the military started to round-up those identified as potentially the most dangerous, treating them as civilian prisoners of war or "enemy aliens." President Roosevelt authorized this action under the Alien Enemies Act of 1798. My father was one of more than 17,000 Japanese immigrants, along with nearly 15,000 additional immigrants of German, Italian, and "other" descent whom the U.S. government confined during World War II in Department of Justice internment camps. This was soon followed by a massive U.S. military action, authorized under Executive Order 9066, that forced into concentration camps approximately 120,000 *Nikkei,* almost all living on the U.S. mainland. *Nikkei* included all people of Japanese descent who emigrated from Japan to the United States and their citizen descendants. My family would be swept up in this mass incarceration of innocent *Nikkei*—citizens and noncitizens alike—and imprisoned in American concentration camps.

No one in my family remembers the exact time on that fateful morning, but it was pitch dark outside. Mama, who almost always woke up early, was still asleep when a loud banging on our front door woke her up. She answered the door in her robe. Six men from the FBI and Seattle Police stormed into the house, pushing Mama aside. Their loud voices woke my sister Nobu, but she stayed in her bedroom upstairs, wondering what the intrusion was about.

Apparently, the agents were looking for my papa, searching every room until they found him in bed, still asleep. They shook him awake and ordered him to get dressed. One agent watched Papa closely, glaring at him. He even followed Papa's every move as Papa uncomfortably went through his morning routine.

Other agents ransacked closets, overturned drawers, and generally made a mess of each room. Two agents began to ascend the stairs to the second floor. Mama shouted up to my sisters in Japanese, *"Hayaku! Hayaku! Kimono kinasai! Hayaku!"* ("Hurry! Hurry! Get dressed! Hurry!") She knew Nobu and Kazu were still in their pajamas, so Mama must have been trying to save them from embarrassment.

As soon as the agents heard Mama shout in Japanese—the language of the enemy—they immediately bounded up the rest of the stairs drawing their guns. My sisters were terrified as strange men burst into their bedroom. Nobu thought the FBI agents looked menacing with their guns in their hands, brandishing their weapons in a threatening way. Kazu shouted in English, "Get out! Get out!"

Kazu was mighty courageous that morning of her eleventh birthday! Yet, inwardly she shook from fright as she watched an agent carefully search the pockets of her dresses hanging in the closet. Nobu froze when one agent showed her his gun and asked, "Does your father have one of these?"

Before that day, the only guns Nobu had ever seen were in the toy box. In these terrifying minutes, Nobu was subdued, which I thought was unusual for her.

In all the chaos, one of the FBI agents realized Mama didn't speak English. He ordered Kazu, as the eldest child, to serve as an interpreter. The other FBI agents continued to ransack the house, never mentioning a search warrant. Kazu was stunned and repulsed as she watched an agent in the kitchen sift through the rice bin, and flour and sugar canisters with unwashed hands. My parents did not know what they were looking for, and the men never bothered to explain.

I don't know when I woke up but I felt a general sense of commotion and tension in the household. At five years old, I was an outside observer. No one seemed to notice me as I stared silently, invisible. Even the baby, Midori, wailed loudly the whole time. We stood by in our pajamas, helpless and vulnerable, as these strangers invaded and raided our home.

The agents confiscated Mama's prayer book and her handwritten telephone book because they were in Japanese. A short while later, the agents appeared elated to find Papa's valued traditional Japanese swords that were stored high in the closet and pushed far back for safekeeping from the children. They also found Papa's longbow, which was unstrung at the time so the kids could play with it without harm. These treasures came from Papa's family in Japan—a family of archers. Archery was one sport that Papa had excelled in.

When the FBI agents were finished searching our home, two men grabbed Papa and pinned him between them as they whisked him out of the house into a waiting car. Papa was not even given a moment to say goodbye to his family. No one told Mama where they were taking Papa. As the cars with Papa and the agents pulled away, we all watched, side by side, through the living room window.

Kazu glanced at Mama who looked frozen, her mind somewhere else. Immediately, fear gripped Kazu as she panicked, wondering what would become of our family. Nobu burst into uncontrollable sobs so strong she had problems breathing. She even wondered if it was possible for a person to choke and actually die from crying too hard. By all accounts, I was there at the window, too, but I have no direct recollection of Papa being taken away.

Not long after the car pulled away, Nobu stopped sobbing and turned her attention to our baby sister, Midori, who was screeching. Nobu had a hard time trying to quiet down Midori. Amid the stunned confusion of Papa being taken away, my family realized that I had disappeared. When Mama and my older sisters recovered somewhat from their shock, they began looking for me, calling my name. I could hear them, but for some reason I couldn't call out and answer.

After a frantic search, they finally found me crying in the corner of the living room, shaking beneath a pile of blankets thrown on the floor when the agents ransacked our home. Once my family found me, they forgot about my trauma. Once again, each of us became encased in our own emotional upheaval and the sudden absence of Papa.

In later years, I heard many family stories about that day and what each family member experienced. Recounting that day, I asked Nobu if we actually ate birthday cake in spite of Papa being taken away. Nobu couldn't remember, but Kazu definitely recalled that her birthday celebration was cancelled. In fact, it was Kazu herself who asked Mama to cancel the occasion and Mama nodded in agreement without any comment. The birthday cake never made it to the oven that day. Apparently, even I, considered a champion complainer, did not complain that day.

Later that afternoon, Mama sent Kazu to the Immigration and Naturalization Service (INS) building in Seattle, a little more than a mile from our house. Kazu was to take Papa his pajamas and other necessities. It was strange that Mama knew Papa would need pajamas when Papa himself was quite sure he would be released in time to join the family for dinner and birthday cake. But then again, Papa was always an optimist, while Mama considered herself to be a realist.

Mama put a pack of Papa's favorite Chesterfield cigarettes in the package along with pajamas, a toothbrush, shaver, a book, and snacks. Funny, the only things I remember are the cigarettes. And that's about all I remember about Kazu's errand that day.

Kazu had a long solitary walk on her eleventh birthday. Reflecting on that time, I wondered, *How did she know where the INS building was located?* It was pretty much a straight shot to the INS building from our house, but still, it was a mystery how she knew where to go. Years later, Kazu herself couldn't recall how she knew the way. Any thoughts of birthday cake and celebrating her special day were far from Kazu's concerns. She was worried about Papa. When Kazu arrived at the INS building where Papa was jailed, the guards told her to leave the package with them and they would give it to Papa. Kazu refused. She told them, "My mother specifically told me to hand this directly to my father."

Nearby there was an *Issei* woman—first generation Japanese in the U.S.— pleading in Japanese to see her husband. She had medication that he needed to take. Kazu helped her by translating her plea into English for the guards. Both Kazu and the woman ended up in chairs, waiting. Three different guards approached Kazu, each one suggesting that she

Kazu. This photo was taken for her eleventh birthday to send to Papa.

leave the package and go home before it got too dark. Later, when Kazu returned home, she told us, "I put on my stubborn face, held on tightly to the package, and continued to wait it out."

One of the guards must have had kids or felt sorry for Kazu sitting there so long, patiently waiting. Whatever the reason, this particular guard quietly came up to Kazu and just said, "Follow me."

Kazu followed him through a series of gates that the guards opened and slammed shut after the nice guard and Kazu passed through. Kazu was intimidated and had grim thoughts of maybe being punished for her willful insistence. The possibility of even being murdered entered her mind. She thought, *No one will find me here.*

She was beginning to regret her determination. Finally, they reached the last gate. There were two guards and one asked, "Who is your father? Is he the fat Takahashi, or the skinny Takahashi?"

Immediately, Kazu said, "The fat Takahashi."

One guard left and the other two guards engaged in subdued conversation while Kazu waited. Then, from around the corner Papa emerged and walked toward Kazu. She ran and hugged him with no restraint. In that moment, Kazu felt pure joy and a lot of relief. Then, she handed Papa the package just as Mama had instructed. Papa immediately gave the package to the guard and then sat down with Kazu on his lap. They did not talk long. Kazu tried to act brave, but she was so scared. Later, she told us she had a feeling that Papa was going to be gone for a long time. "It's amazing how you can feel joyful one second," Kazu explained, "and have it all melt away so quickly."

When Kazu left the INS building, she cried most of the way home. She didn't notice if the *Issei* woman with the medication for her husband was still waiting or not. Kazu worried, asking herself, *Who will take care of us? Without Papa making money for us to live on, how are we going to avoid hunger?*

Kazu wondered if she could get a job and provide for the family needs. By the time she got home, she was too tired physically and too emotionally spent to talk. She went straight to her room and cried through the night.

Late that night, I got out of bed to use the bathroom. That's when I heard Mama crying in the living room by herself. This was the second time in my life I had seen Mama cry. The first time had been a few months earlier when *Obaachan* (Grandmother) died. That was when I learned that grown-ups cried, too. But on this night Mama's crying was different. It sounded frightening. I wanted to hug Mama, but I could not bring myself to approach her. I'm not sure if I wanted to comfort her or to be comforted *by* her. Maybe both. I would never forget that moment in my childhood when I realized the adults could also be scared and broken. Many times since that day, I have regretted not going to Mama.

Forever after, that day would be remembered not only as Kazu's eleventh birthday, but even more as being the first day of a prolonged, sorrow-laden experience for our whole family.

Many times I have wondered, *What was going through Papa's mind on that frightful day?* As time passed, Mama and the girls seemed to have even more to discuss about that unforgettable day.

Years later, we prodded Papa to tell us about his incarceration experience after he was taken from our midst. Papa rarely had much to say, and getting Papa to say something new became almost a game for us daughters. It was like a baby learning how to talk. His vocabulary was limited to one or two words and then slowly expanded to more and more words. His thoughts and memories on other matters were normal, but he faltered when trying to talk about being torn away from his family and locked up as an "enemy alien." As he shared more of his memories, Papa also shared more of his emotions that he had hidden behind his words. He was always a verbal man, so it was even stranger to witness his struggle recalling and sharing these stories.

Papa did tell us that during his ride with the FBI agents to the INS building, he resolved to be patient. Papa knew he had done nothing wrong, so he believed he would be released soon after a short interview. He thought of a few minor infractions that he had committed, but it didn't seem possible that these small violations would be the cause for punishment of any consequence. Papa remembered staying out past the curfew on a few occasions, double parking his car and getting a ticket, and the time he spoke up for one of his workers at the cannery who may have been involved in poor judgment regarding a fellow worker. Papa said he searched his memory for any action on his part that may have led the authorities to question his adherence to the law. He could only conclude that the FBI apprehending him was simply a mistake. He thought, *Everything will turn out good once I am cleared. I won't be here for long.*

Papa said that by late afternoon on that first day, while sitting in the jail, one of the prisoners locked up in the same large cell, gently shook my father's shoulder. He told Papa there were many fellow prisoners who were in grief, tormented, worrying about their families. He also asked Papa, "Could you try to not snore so loud? You're disturbing them even more!" Papa wanted to accommodate his fellow prisoners, but staying awake so as not to snore was a difficult task. Convinced he would be released soon from custody, Papa found it difficult to stay awake and returned to napping. He gave sleeping without snoring a yeoman's try.

Unfortunately, by the end of the long day Papa's optimism was greatly shaken. All the prisoners were ordered to undress. The men were shocked and humiliated at having to stand naked in front of the guards. When Papa told me that story many years later, I did not push him for more information. He needed some privacy. I could imagine how hard it must've been for these men to hold on to their dignity in such a situation.

From his cell, Papa could look out the jail window and almost see our house across the valley. Many of Papa's fellow inmates openly wept. Even Papa admitted to feeling teary. As dinnertime came and went on the first day in jail, and he was still being held, Papa wondered how much his girls missed him. He wondered how much longer it would take for his jailers to correct their mistake and release him back to his family.

Papa had no idea that it would be almost two years before he was reunited with his family.

12

CHAPTER 2

ALL TEARS ARE SALTY

At the time President Roosevelt signed Executive Order 9066, my family was not aware of this government action, or its consequences. We were completely distracted with Papa being taken away by the FBI. However, before long, we would understand the full implications of that day, February 19, 1942, and its impact on Japanese American communities across the nation—but especially on the West Coast.

We were focused on Papa's detention at the INS facility. Exactly how long my father was held at the INS jail is not something our family's collective memory could determine years later. We were all in a fog at that point. It had to be between February 21, the day they took Papa away, and May 1, the day the rest of the family left for the Puyallup temporary concentration camp.

When we learned the whole family would be able to visit Papa in the INS facility, we were delighted. Because I was barely five years old in 1942, my memories of this day are sketchy at best. For my eldest sister, Kazu, this would be her second visit to the INS building. She had reservations about going back, but she overcame her apprehension for the chance to see Papa. Kazu figured that at least this time she would not be alone.

During the visit, Mama and Papa were in a pleasant and humorous mood. Everyone tried to be cheerful and comforting to one another. We even shared with the guards some of the sweet snacks we brought. Our talk was lively and optimistic. When the visit came to an end and we were almost through the goodbyes, a strange thing happened.

Mama and my sisters had gotten ahead of me as we were leaving. I was lingering, trying to extend my time with Papa. The guard who was waiting to close the gate behind us decided to tease me. Before I could catch up with my family, he slammed the gate closed in front of me and announced, "Now, you are a prisoner and you will have to stay here."

Mama, my sisters, Papa, and even the guard were all surprised by my reaction. Rather than react with fear, I flew back into Papa's arms and cheered, "Oh boy, I get to stay with Papa!"

As I snuggled in Papa's arms, Mama's expression changed from shock to silent welling tears. There in Papa's lap, time seemed to freeze. Then Mama saw the expression change on the teasing guard's face—from the exaggerated grimace of a bully into a sorrowful look of a man struggling to hold back tears. Mama saw a tear fall from the guard's eyes and run down his face. This tenderness moved Mama, and she found comfort and hope in his tears.

Years later, whenever Mama shared this story, I would smile and feel that same hope. All tears are salty, and warm hearts come encased in all skin colors.

I don't know how Mama learned the date and time Papa was going to be moved from the INS building and relocated to a site unknown to us. When that day came, Mama combed my hair with particular care; she braided it carefully and put ribbons on the ends. All of us dressed in our finest outfits and hurried to the King Street train station in downtown Seattle. We stood behind a chain-link fence at the station, trying to stay warm, waiting for Papa to appear. There were other families anxiously waiting, too. More people helped block off some of the cold.

Finally, the bus arrived. My two older sisters immediately spotted Papa among all the other men getting off the bus and shouted to him. In recalling that day, Kazu thought there were possibly three buses allowed through the gate. About a dozen men got off the bus before Kazu and Nobu caught sight of Papa. They kept track of him amidst the thirty to forty men who got off each bus. "Papa, Papa, we're here. Over here, Papa!" my sisters yelled as loudly as they could.

Papa spotted us right away, thanks to my sisters' yelling. The fence was tall and sturdy, keeping us from running into his arms. Several menacing-looking soldiers with bayoneted rifles and sidearm guns were conspicuous among the imprisoned men.

Papa considered approaching one of the guards to seek permission to meet with his family behind the fence. But on second thought, he decided to just slowly approach the fence and be ready to stop if he was ordered away from the fence. Papa was tense. Aware that the guards might yell at him at any moment, he walked

ILLUSTRATION: MITS KATAYAMA

slowly toward the fence. Getting shot without a prior warning was not probable, but it was still possible. He was actually surprised he made it all the way without being stopped. My sisters immediately bombarded Papa with questions, both talking at the same time in their excitement:

"Papa, where are they taking you?"

"Papa, how long will you be gone?"

"Will they let us join you?"

"Did you tell them you did nothing wrong, Papa?"

"How will we find you, Papa?

"Did you tell them we need you?"

"What will happen to us, Papa?"

Papa was concentrating so much on getting to the fence, he was totally unprepared to respond to the barrage of questions my sisters shouted at him. He regretted not thinking of what he might say to his kids. Papa looked to Mama for help, but he knew immediately she would be of no help. Tears streamed down her face as she watched her daughters reach for their papa.

The fence prohibited much physical contact, but my sisters' outstretched hands grabbed Papa like they would never let go. Just then, an announcement came over the speaker telling the INS "travelers" to begin boarding the train. I imagine Papa felt relieved of the frantic pressure my sisters posed. He managed to mumble something to us quickly, like, *"Mama no yukoto kikun da yo."* ("Mind your Mama.")

Then he turned to Mama and said, *"Tanomu yo!"* (Roughly, "I'm counting on you.")

Then, Papa turned toward the train and steadily walked away. My sisters kept calling to him.

"Papa, Papa, don't leave us!"

"Don't go, Papa."

"How will we find you, Papa?"

"I'm scared, Papa!"

The walk to the train covered more time than his quick stop by the fence with his family. The guards hurried the men along. They weren't rude to the prisoners, but they were also intent on filling up the seats on the train quickly. It was only a few minutes and then Papa was gone.

When the train pulled away from the station and we wiped the tears from our faces, we began to feel the cold of that day. Only baby Midori seemed to be snuggly wrapped up and warm in her blankets. Nobu said it was funny that she didn't feel the cold while Papa was with us; only when he left did the cold become uncomfortable. They all agreed that Papa seemed to be his normal self when he walked toward us, the familiar slight bounce to his walk. Many of the other men seemed tired and lost. But when Papa turned his back and walked away from his family, it was amazing how much Papa had changed—as if he had turned into an old man. "It was like he left a trail of himself oozing on the cement," recalled Kazu.

After our brief exchange with Papa at the train station, we did not see him for two years. During our own subsequent imprisonment, my sisters and mother often recounted that day. They talked about how Papa looked, what he said, what he might have meant to say had he had more time, what he didn't say—even, what they would have liked him to say. For a long time, Mama and my older sisters guessed how long it would be before we saw Papa again. No one ever mentioned out loud the possibility that we might never see him again.

As time passed, Papa receded from my consciousness. I found these conversations about Papa, including the day at the train station, fading beyond my ability to participate. For the next two years, I felt cheated. I longed for a father.

When my father finally told me his version of the train station story, he was 88 years old. By then, Papa was almost totally deaf, but he told me that he could still clearly hear his girls calling to him across four decades of time. He told me when he heard our cries that day, it was the first time it occurred to him he might never see his family again. Papa said when he walked away, he wanted to turn and look back. He wanted to take one last look at his family—an image he could treasure. But Papa did not look back. He told me he decided he couldn't afford this luxury, afraid he would be unable to keep his composure. The melancholic look on Papa's face the day he shared his memory still brings tears to my eyes.

Mama and Papa with relatives and friends. Nobu
is sitting on Mama's lap and Papa stands behind
Mama. Kazu is the middle child in front.

CHAPTER 3

THE ALL AMERICAN FAMILY?

*M*y parents, Hisako Takahashi (Mama) and Masao Takahashi (Papa) met in Seattle, Washington, married, and raised four daughters in the Northwest. Maybe Papa would have welcomed a son by the time I was born, but that was not meant to be. Mama tried to make Papa a little happy by naming me, the third daughter, Masako, which is the female version of Papa's name, Masao. He still wanted a boy, but mostly, Papa was very happy to have healthy daughters.

From the beginning of their marriage, one thing Mama and Papa had in common was an extraordinary love of children and their desire to have a family. Mama had seven miscarriages before their first baby, Toshiko, was born. Unfortunately, this baby girl was weak at birth and died a few months after she was born. Both parents were devastated, but it seemed Mama especially had difficulty speaking about this death.

When I was older, I remember being very moved when Mama told me about the Shinto service they had for Baby Toshiko. Mama said she felt a strong urge to "pick up the baby and run away." Mama explained that the feeling didn't make sense, but it was compelling. Instead, Mama stayed in the room, pulled up a deep inner strength, and forced herself to focus and not run away. Mama made it through the chanting, but she lost her self-control when the funeral director put Toshiko's little body into a suitcase to take it back to the mortuary. Mama couldn't believe her eyes. She began protesting, "No! No! No!"

PHOTO: NAKAGAWA PRIVATE COLLECTION

Mama and her first child, Baby Toshiko, who died.

Mama told me she couldn't bear to think of Toshiko being put into a suitcase. When I heard her story, I thought, *This is tough, Mama! Gambare!* (Hang in there!) To this day, picturing Mama as a young mother running away with the body of her first baby makes me so sad.

Two years after the death of Baby Toshiko, their daughter Kazuko was born in 1931. Mama and Papa were not only happy beyond belief, they were also very anxious to see that Kazu remained healthy and vigorous. Mama and Papa both were obsessive parents. They called her "Kachan" or "Kazu," a nickname that seemed to fit her well. The Japanese "one hundred day celebration" and the "one year celebration" for Kazu were truly joyful occasions for Mama and Papa as they watched their daughter thrive.

By the time they were celebrating Kazu's first birthday, they were already delighted to learn another child was on the way. Nobuye (shortened to Nobu) was born in 1932, another healthy daughter. Between Nobu's birth and mine, Mama had another miscarriage, but my parents were determined to have more children. I joined the family in 1937, and our baby sister, Midori, completed our family in 1940. She was born prematurely and required an incubator to help her survive. Midori stayed in the hospital for about a month beyond Mama's stay. The family waited anxiously before being allowed to bring Midori home.

Mako on her first birthday.

As the family grew, my parents' vision of raising a number of precious "princesses" had to be abandoned. For starters, the first two daughters were quite different. Kazu was sweet, charming, and polite—what her parents considered a "proper child." But Nobu was full of mischievous antics and constant energy. She was inquisitive, adventurous, and ready to take on a fight—physical or verbal—at a moment's notice. Mama and Papa were often perplexed how these two daughters from the same family could be so different.

Kazu charmed everyone, but she charmed Papa in particular. For example, she was certainly not the first child in the world who wanted the moon, however, Kazu may have been the first to convince her father to literally help her catch the moon. One night when Kazu was about five years old, Papa and Kazu actually climbed up to the attic of the house carrying a long rope with them. They both sat on the small window-sill for hours hoping to catch the moon with their lasso. Kazu stubbornly waited with Papa—who had great patience—to bring in the big prize. When sleep finally proved to be the victor over Kazu, Mama and Papa carefully lowered their sleeping daughter from the attic and put her to bed.

The next morning, Mama praised Kazu for being such a good person for leaving the moon in the sky so that many other people could enjoy it along with Kazu. When I was older and first heard the story about my oldest sister, I could almost picture a proud smile on Kazu's face as Papa winked at her.

On the other hand, if Nobu was in the same situation, I envision her with the rope in *her* hands, and I like to think Nobu actually would have captured the moon! Nobu seemed fearless in her adventures and nothing seemed beyond her reach—not even the moon.

One of our family's favorite stories about Nobu was the time she noticed Kazu sitting quietly in the back end of the school bus, tears streaming down her cheeks. Of course, Nobu wanted to know why her sister was crying. Nobu was stunned to learn that Mieko, a well-known bully girl, was pinching Kazu. Nobu couldn't believe that Kazu's only visible response was the quiet tears. Immediately, Nobu jumped into action. She pounced on the offending girl, gave Mieko a hard and long pinch, and yelled at her, "If you ever touch Kazu again, I will have to pinch you even harder and longer than when you pinched Kazu. So you better stay far *far away.*"

Nobu was quite sure that this incident would find its way to the school administrators, and she was prepared to state her case as necessary in order to protect her sister. She was full of righteous indignation but still worried that the teachers might not agree with her position. In the end, Nobu was never called upon to give her account of the incident. She was relieved, but truth be told, Nobu was somewhat disappointed, too.

Every day after school, my two older sisters visited the new baby and Mama at Providence Hospital which was near the school. They continued to visit Baby Midori even after Mama came home. When Mama finally brought Midori home, I was not impressed. It seemed everyone who saw Midori smiled and made some comment about how cute she was. I wondered, *Are they looking at the same baby I am looking at? This baby is far from cute. Let's face it, she is ugly.*

From my perspective, Midori's skin looked greenish, wrinkled, and very dry. Her diapers were miserably stinky and her cries unbearably loud, long, and screechy. I did surmise that mentioning these unfortunate flaws would not be well received, so I did not say much. I didn't think I was being jealous, I just hoped the baby would become better looking with time. She did.

Our modest rental house in Seattle was within the Japantown, or *Nihonmachi*, border. One block away from the street we lived on, Hiawatha Place, two major streets intersected. Dearborn Street, originally called

PHOTO: NAKAGAWA PRIVATE COLLECTION

Mako's sisters, Kazu and Nobu, taking part in *Shichi-Go-San*, a rite of passage for Japanese children to celebrate good health.

Mikado Street until 1895, and Rainier Avenue was a busy intersection in Seattle's Japantown. Prior to World War II, Japanese-owned businesses flourished in this area.

Papa had many jobs during his years in America, but his current job as a cannery foreman at an Alaskan fish company was quite lucrative for an immigrant. When Papa began working for white bosses in America, it was not unusual for them to tag Japanese immigrant workers with a Western name rather than bother to learn and pronounce the workers' Japanese names. Papa's work name was "Tom." Even Mama was given the name "Rose" by white people she knew. Interestingly, many of the immigrants often had Western names, while their children, as natural born U.S. citizens, often had only names of Japanese derivative. My sisters and I had Japanese names even though their white fellow workers and neighbors generally called our parents Rose and Tom.

Midori and I stayed home with Mama during the day while Kazu and Nobu attended the local Catholic Maryknoll School. Papa was often gone from home setting up one thing or another related to his job. On a few occasions, Papa took me to the nursery school at the Maryknoll School to help me "socialize." I hated it. The hoards of children frightened me and the teachers looked strange in their odd clothes. We were to call the teachers "Sisters." When I heard that all I could think was, *They aren't my sisters!*

One day while I was visiting the nursery school, I put off asking to go to the bathroom. When I finally asked for permission, it was too late. I dribbled on the way to the bathroom. Sister Madeline made me take a paper towel and wipe up what she called "the mistake." I thought, *Mama would never have asked me to do such a horrid task. That was a job for the adults.*

As a result, I visualized Sister Madeline as a monster and I would not cooperate. When I was at the nursery school, I refused to nap, I refused to sing, and I even refused to smile. I suppose you could call this the first of many organized protests I would participate in throughout my life.

We added *Obaachan* (Grandmother) to our household not long after Midori was born, so she would have better access to the hospital. *Obaachan* had been diagnosed with lung cancer and needed my parents' help. With Mama and Papa, plus four daughters and *Obaachan*, our two-and-a-half bedroom house was snug. I did not pay much attention to a crowded house—it was all I knew. I also did not pay much attention to the adult talk, but it was hard not to notice the serious tone of some discussions. When the adults were in the middle of their talks, I simply left the house and made it down to the sidewalk with my new rollerskates I had just gotten for my fifth birthday. I thought I was quite brave to skate alone because I had been told I could get hurt when I fell. I was determined to get as good as my big sisters on rollerskates and I needed to practice.

Before long, I gave up on rollerskating. Instead, I focused on trying to become "special." Nobody noticed. I saw both of my older sisters as fortunate to be so well endowed with their attributes, including experts at rollerskating. I just knew they were leaders, but each in her own way. I wondered, *What could I do to be special, too?*

My sisters said I was "cute," and for being so little, I already showed signs of being a talented classical Japanese dancer, but I longed for more. When I learned I had been born in a real hospital, this became one of the few things that made me feel special—different than Kazu and Nobu who had been born at home with the help of a midwife. When I came along, four-and-a-half years later, my mother gave birth in a hospital. I felt "special"—

that is, until Midori was born some three years later. Now, the two of us had been born in a hospital. Unfortunately, Baby Midori even outdid me in the specialness category because she was born on a special day called "Columbus Day." In addition, Midori only weighed four pounds at birth, so she was special even *before* leaving the hospital. My sisters bragged that the new baby was truly special weighing only four pounds. I wondered, *How can I compete with three highly "special" sisters.*

As far as good looks in our family, sister Kazu was the beauty. I admired Kazu's beauty and Nobu's brains. The problem I faced was that my two older sisters had the beauty and the brains, so there didn't seem to be any accolade of comparable worth left for me. As I grew, Mama often talked of my having artistic talent and a sensitive nature, but at the time, those qualities seemed to be poor substitutes for beauty or brains. I wouldn't doubt that Mama made up these traits just to make me happy. For certain, from an early age I was envious of my sisters, but I was proud of them, too. These thoughts about my place in the family preoccupied much of my time while the adult world unraveled into World War II.

Overall, I was oblivious to the increasing worries among the adults. Their concerns were over my head. I was protected from the brewing anti-Japanese sentiments in the United States. Years later as an adult, I read that people who live through major historical events often don't recognize their personal involvement in the occurrence. I can attest to that.

As a child, I was much more interested in roller skating and being special, mostly oblivious to adult issues such as banks freezing the accounts of Japanese customers or a curfew being placed on German, Italian, and Japanese nationals, and even Japanese American citizens. I didn't understand why Japanese neighbors were holding "evacuation sales," or routinely being referred to as "Japs" in the news or by angry whites. I did not pay much attention to the adult talk, but it was hard not to notice the serious—sometimes combative—tone of their discussions.

I did surmise from bits of adult talk I overheard that we were to move soon. No one seemed to know where we were moving or *why* we were moving. No one seemed happy about this move. My older sisters moaned about having to move away from baseball playing with the neighbor kids. I would have to give up my rollerskating sessions. Mama loathed the thought of giving up her garden. She grew the best peaches in the world; they were so good I could taste those peaches in my dreams. Maintaining the yard, including the fruit trees and the vegetable garden, was one of Mama's special joys. There was much nervousness and many questions among the family members—far more questions than answers.

In many ways, our family was pretty much the "all-American family," yet we had undeniable Japanese ways and lifestyles. As Japanese Americans, we were also subjected to the ever-present mainstream Americanism that was tainted with white American privilege. Much later in my life, I would understand that whatever the grand and lofty ideals of Americanism were,

Papa, left, next to Mama, along with friends before the war.

there was, and still continues to be, a gap between American ideals and American practices.

In time, I would see that Japanese Americans were constantly reminded that we are different, and often demeaned and discredited by the white world. But in 1942, I was a five-year-old American kid focused on my rollerskates and being special, oblivious to older people's increasing worries.

CHAPTER 4

WHAT TO LEAVE BEHIND?

Not long after Papa left on the train, we began to hear rumors that the next round of people to be incarcerated would be *all people* of Japanese descent living in the Western United States. Many *Niseis* (second generation Japanese living in the U.S. and citizens by birthright) strongly opposed the suggestion that they would be imprisoned. There seemed to be general acceptance that the *Isseis* (the first generation of Japanese in the U.S.) were vulnerable to government incarceration but not the *Niseis*—they were U.S. citizens! The Japanese community believed that the *Niseis* would be protected by the United States' Constitution which guarantees their civil liberties. They did not believe the U.S. government would deprive them of life, liberty, or property without the due process of law.

Most *Niseis* were shocked that their government would actually imprison them. They couldn't fathom that their government was truly going to incarcerate *all* Japanese aliens and "non-aliens." Many people questioned exactly who was a "non-alien." As U.S. citizens, many *Niseis* considered the government's description of them as "non-aliens" to be an unbelievable betrayal. Many were angry and bitter, but most people in the Japanese American community couldn't afford the time to lament and argue over the expulsion from their homes and communities.

On April 24, 1942, the local military posted public "relocation notices" for *all* people of Japanese ancestry, including U.S. citizens. The relocation notices to "all persons of Japanese ancestry" produced more questions than answers. In addition to the military instructions posted on telephone poles and in other public places, specific information pertaining to the actual move included the following items of key interest:

2. Evacuees must carry with them on departure for the Assembly Center, the following property:
    a) Bedding and linens (no mattress) for each member of the family
    b) Toilet articles for each member of the family
    c) Extra clothing for each member of the family
    d) Sufficient knives, forks, spoons, plates, bowls and cups for each member of the family
    (e) Essential personal effects for each member of the family
        The size and number of packages is limited to that which can be carried by the individual or family group
3. No pets of any kind will be permitted

The "no pets" rule caused havoc with many people. If a family had beloved animal companions, they had to find a place for them within a week. Mama was born in the year of the tiger and claimed that people born in the "tiger year" did not do well caring for pets, so our family did not have the added heartbreak of parting with a loved pet. We did feel sorry for people who were forced to leave their pets behind, particularly their dogs. Many times my sisters had begged Mama to let them get a dog. Now, this was one less thing we had to leave behind, already giving up so much.

But for many, the "no pets" rule caused great sorrow for the owners and for their animals. One family well known in the Japanese community on Bainbridge Island, Mr. and Mrs. Moji, had their dog, King, who was their pride and joy. The Mojis had no children, so their dog was the center of their life. In turn, King was completely bonded to the Mojis. When they had to leave King behind, he stopped eating, grieving for his family. The new caretakers tried their best to get King to eat, but the dog refused. Eventually, King lost weight and became so weak, he died. I can't help but assume he died from a broken heart.

The set date for our departure was May 1, 1942, which only left seven days for Japanese families to take care of an unbelievable amount of preparations and work. The military labeled this an "evacuation," or "relocation," but in truth it was the "forced removal" or "expulsion" of *Nikkei*—all persons of Japanese descent—from their homes. There was very little time to take care of matters and comply with the government's travel orders. In many cases, targeted people were given only a week to handle their business affairs, family affairs, and to desperately look for people to watch and care for their crops and farms. For most, this would mean financial ruin.

Quickly, people had to dispose of their homes, their household goods, clothing, anything they couldn't carry —or find a way to store their things. Families sold items at "evacuation sales" for little or nothing. Greedy consumers acted like vultures, looking for items they might be able to purchase at ridiculously low bargain prices. When I was older, I tried to make sense of this frenzy that made people exploit their neighbors who were forced to leave the area. I wondered, *Didn't they understand that they were profiting at the cost of the injustice being perpetrated on the* Nikkei *victims?*

There was a lot of hustle and bustle in our home between the time the order was posted and the date we were to leave. We could hear Mama hammering away into the very late hours of night. We didn't know where she got the lumber, but she was making crates into which she would place some of our precious possessions. The only item that we remember Mama putting into the crate was her sewing machine, her most precious possession of all. She got little sleep. Most of the people in the *Nikkei* community suffered from lack of sleep.

"There is little time for grief," Mama said. "We will hold our tears for the future when we have the time to weep. For now, we have work to do."

Mama sorted through family valuables—clothing, tools, *everything*—deciding what to bring, what to toss, what to store, and what to give away. She hardly put together family meals during this time because she was too busy preparing for our departure.

My concern was for my priceless musical box. Uncle Roy (Mama's brother, Kiyoshi) gave it to me for my birthday a few months earlier. Immediately after tearing the wrapping off my birthday present, I knew this was a special gift, indeed. The music box stood about ten inches tall in the shape of a church steeple. The design on the face was of stained glass windows. When I turned the little crank at the bottom of this music box, the most heavenly organ music came out, transporting me to a world I never knew existed. The adults smiled as I turned the crank and shared the magic music with them. They looked like they enjoyed it, but not one of them seemed transported by the music as much as I was.

To my surprise, at the end of my birthday no one came to remove this treasure from my five-year-old hands for safekeeping. I was delighted to be allowed to keep the music box with me. I was also baffled that the adults seemed to completely miss the priceless nature of this most fantastic gift. How could they be immune to the magical power of the music it played? For three months, my music box was always with me—that is, until we had to leave our home.

Mama was too busy to worry about anything beyond getting the family ready to leave. Even after our belongings were somewhat cleared out, the house had to be cleaned in preparation for the next occupants. The FBI had also taken Mama's brother Kiyoshi away, so Mama was left with no adult help as she prepared to leave with her four young children in tow. We were not alone; we had other friends who were in the same predicament as they prepared for the forced removal from their homes.

The thought of moving to this new place that no one seemed to know where or what it was, seemed to pale when I thought about having to leave my treasured music box behind. Mama explained that we could only take what we could carry. Mama had to carefully determine what was a "necessity" for our family. She also had to make sure we were able to carry what we brought, obeying the government's regulations. There was no room for my music box. In my world, nothing could be more cruel than making me abandon my music box.

Kazu, who was barely eleven, was in charge of carrying Midori since the baby was not walking yet. Midori was developmentally slow due to her premature birth. At nine years old, Nobu had quite a load to carry as well, plus the added charge of watching over me. I had to carry a big load of diapers for my baby sister. Mama was overloaded with a mountain of belongings. It must have taken a superhuman effort for her to keep everything from falling on to the rain-drenched sidewalk as we walked to a designated loading area. Years later, Kazu recalled that day, saying, "I cried as I walked to the place the bus would be loading us. The baby was heavy, but I had to keep holding her while we waited for the buses. My arms hurt so badly I thought I would permanently damage them."

Kazu said at one point she looked over at Mama with the idea of asking for some relief from carrying Midori. The ground was too wet to put the baby down, but one look at Mama— overloaded herself—and Kazu knew relief was impossible. Mama could hardly carry what she already had. So, Kazu cried silently from the pain in her arms. She also cried silently for the farewell to the home and friends she loved. She was leaving so much behind and she was facing a completely unknown future.

For me, I couldn't get over having to leave my precious music box behind. I complained about the loss of my music box for a long time. I couldn't give up the grief of losing it. I just knew my loss was the biggest loss of all. Little did I know.

As we walked away from our home into the unknown, I kept wondering, *Why do we have to move? Why are diapers more important than my music box with music from heaven? Can't we leave the baby behind?*

CHAPTER 5

FIRST PRISON CAMP, PUYALLUP

When the buses finally arrived at the designated place near our house in Seattle, we knew it would take us to a destination unknown and frightening. Kazu was somewhat distracted in the midst of everything going on, including the pain of having to say goodbye to friends who came to see her off. Her arms ached from holding baby Midori, who felt heavier by the minute. Kazu was greatly relieved when the buses pulled up to the sidewalk. She quickly said a last goodbye to her friends, boarded the closest bus and took the nearest available seat. Kazu's arms hurt so badly she worried she might be crippled for life, never regaining her normal strength.

Because of the steady rain, neither Kazu nor Mama was able to put their bundles on the ground during the wait. Kazu wished the pain of losing her friends would counteract the pain in her arms, but she ached inside and out. Glancing out the window, Kazu saw that a few of the guards were helping some people load their belongings on to the buses. Kazu hoped Mama got some help, too. She could only imagine how it was for Mama and *her* aching arms. Mama was quite a petite woman, always weighing less than a hundred pounds. Yet, Mama somehow managed to carry overwhelming bundles. On this day, Mama was a sight to behold. Fierce determination was chiseled on her face—a look that said she would do *all* that was needed to protect her four young daughters. Kazu told me years later that she admired Mama's fortitude, and that day, she definitely felt Mama's pride in her heart.

The buses pulled out to an unknown destination. As Kazu looked out the window, she wondered, *Where are we going? What will happen to us?* She wanted to ask someone who might know the answers to her questions, but everyone seemed absorbed with their own thoughts. People sat quietly as our bus headed south from Seattle and away from home. Even the small children were surprisingly still.

After a little more than an hour, the buses finally passed through the gates where we would be staying, and came to a stop. Obviously, it was time to disembark. We were at the Puyallup Assembly Center (PAC), a temporary facility the government set up to house thousands of *Nikkei* and later distribute them into permanent prison encampments.

Prior to our arrival, government authorities had workers frantically refit the Washington State Fairgrounds in Puyallup to make room for this sudden influx of thousands of people. Barbed-wire fences cordoned off large areas with tarpapered barracks. The interior walls of the barracks were not really walls, but rather thin plywood partitions that did not reach the ceiling.

In fact, there was no "ceiling" for the partitions to reach, just drafty, wood-framed rafters with roofs, and outside walls covered in tarpaper. These buildings had been quickly constructed with no concern for insulation. Within a matter of weeks, the population at the assembly center would explode to more than 7,300 *Nikkei*, our family among them.

We were assigned to "Area A," which turned out to be the parking lot area northeast of the Washington State Fairgrounds. It was surrounded with a barbed-wire fence and manned guard towers at each of the four corners. A few of the new inmates pointed at the guard towers as we entered the camp. My sisters couldn't figure out what the guards were doing and they were intimidated by the presence of these men with guns. Their weapons were clearly visible. Someone used the term "machine guns" and I wondered what a "machine gun" was. I did know enough to feel strange within this busy setting.

After Mama filled out some paperwork, one woman was assigned to our family. She looked friendly enough, but we were hurried into following her as she helped us carry our belongings. It was a long muddy walk from the registration area to our assigned barrack and our family's unit. We saw many people along the way, busy, trying to make their area as livable as possible under the circumstances. Baggage tags, which all family members were required to wear that first day, fluttered from the children's clothing as they all ran about. My baggage tag read #11590 D—our family had been reduced to a number.

Our guide directed Mama to our crude living quarters. The room was about 20' by 20', and one naked light bulb hung down to light the area. There was a single electrical socket and a wood stove. The only places to sit were on the cots, on our suitcases, or on the floor. One small window on the opposite side from the door offered a sliver of natural light and was suppose to improve ventilation, which we would soon find out in the summer heat was near useless. We were provided with four army cots and a blanket for each family member.

When Kazu realized these barracks were to be "home," she wanted to scream. Instead, she and Nobu tried to help Mama get our family situated. They were given four huge canvas bags and told to fill them with straw. Only the early arrivals at the camp got cotton mattresses; every one else had straw-filled coarse bags called straw tick. This was certainly a new experience for my two older sisters, as it was for almost everyone else stuffing the bags to make mattresses. We had four cots in our living area. Mama quickly decided she would sleep with baby Midori and have one of the older girls in a cot on the other side so that Midori would not fall on the floor in the middle of the night. Midori was a restless sleeper, and there were no baby cribs available.

That first day at the camp everyone was bustling about, filled with a mix of confusion, anxiety, anger, frustration, and downright bewilderment with their new predicament. Mama visited the mess hall and the laundry area, anywhere people gathered, so she might get more information. Not knowing what the future held, this quickly festered into frustration. Conjecture and rumors began to run rampant throughout the camp. It did not take long on our first day at Puyallup to realize we were basically in a prison.

My shy and petite mother, under the protection of men most of her life in America, was now thrust into a huge, crowded society as the head of the family. She not only had to cope with the tremendous change in her life routines, but she was expected to protect her young family single-handedly at a time of major turmoil. Somehow, Mama found her inner strength, or what I thought of as her "extra umph" in time of need. This was something we all counted on Mama to have—her ability to find energy when the rest of us were completely exhausted. As far as I know, no one helped her. Everyone else had their own urgent tasks in preparing for what the U.S. government deceptively called "relocation "and "evacuation" to an "assembly center."

Throughout all of this upheaval, Mama's two brothers had taken their own paths amid the disruption and chaos. Uncle Shig had married his girlfriend, Charolette, with little fanfare, and the two of them were incarcerated at Minidoka Concentration Camp, even though Uncle Shig was a U.S. citizen. Uncle Shig was anxious to join the military and when allowed, signed up to serve his country. He was proud to answer the call of the U.S. government, believing it was his primary duty. A number of his close friends were raring to join up, so Uncle Shig left his pregnant wife at Minidoka and began his duties as a soldier. After the war, Uncle Shig admitted that he had gotten caught up in the patriotic fervor.

However, Shig's brother Roy made very different decisions. Unlike his patriotic brother, Roy viewed himself as totally Japanese. So, while Mama was trying to deal with all of us being shipped off to a prison camp, her brother Roy was making himself scarce. His encounters with authority figures were not always smooth or cordial. As helpful as our Uncle Roy was to Mama on many occasions, during this time he deliberately avoided meeting up with our family. He once announced to his friends that the best thing he could do for his family was to try to disappear and not be noticed.

So, Mama was on her own with four young daughters. She met the challenges and adjusted to many changes thrust upon our family. Mama was tough. Along the way, she not only gave support to her daughters, but she offered help to strangers who needed it.

I was just happy to be with my family, even though I was still sad about my music box. Many younger children seemed to have a different experience than the adults. They perceived their new surroundings as comparable to being on a holiday. Parental supervision was minimal since the adults were burdened with so many new responsibilities. The children liked having so many new friends to play with, plus, going to "camp" seemed like an exciting outing at first. For kids of that era, it may have been an adventure just to get on a bus or a train, and go somewhere beyond their neighborhood. Many children from farming families enjoyed being released from their daily farm chores and experiencing new things.

Like me, many of the children were filled with curiosity and excitement as we explored our strange new surroundings. One of the boys told of an adventure he and a couple of friends had. They climbed a mysterious ladder inside a building, which led to another ladder, and this ladder led to a trap door above them. They pushed up the trap door and poked their heads through to see what was there. To their surprise, they saw two soldiers with rifles looking at them. The soldiers were just as surprised as the boys and sternly commanded the boys to "get off the ladder and never climb it again." The boys turned and scrambled back down the ladders as fast they could. They certainly had an exciting story to brag about to the rest of the camp children.

We soon learned privacy was next to impossible both within each family as well as with others in the same barracks. Parents, as well as both male and female children, were crammed into the same small space with no dividers for individual needs within the family. Some families strung blankets to create minimal private areas. There was about a foot gap between the top of the thin plywood partitions and the open rafters. We could easily look into our neighbors' areas by simply standing on something to peer over the divider, or better yet, punch out a knothole.

We heard just about any human sound traveling from one end of the barracks to the other through the open rafters. Crying babies, people playing musical instruments, arguments, laughter, quiet sobs, and all the routine activities of normal living blended into a daily cacophony in the prison camp. At night, snoring neighbors, coughing bouts, teeth grinding, even restless tossing on noisy straw mattresses, were common. I was too young to understand all the night noises. For adults, making love was quite difficult due to the noise produced by the straw, which was noisier than one would guess. Later, I learned that teenage boys delighted in snickering over what they claimed they heard and saw. Some peeked through knotholes in the flimsy partitions, or even looked over the low walls into the quarters of their neighbors. My friend's uncle told us that as a teenager, he learned all he needed to know about sex by peeking into the area of a newly married couple living next to them. These substandard and humiliating living conditions were stressful and dehumanizing for families.

The exposed two-by-four lumber in the barracks was part of the construction for the outer wall. Residents quickly put strips of lumber to use as shelves to hold brushes, combs, toothbrushes, pencils, and an assortment of other small items. The cramped living spaces, combined with no privacy and little to entertain them, resulted in many families spending minimal time within their assigned barracks quarters. There always seemed to be other youngsters waiting to play outside, so my sisters and I were usually playing outside.

Strict regulations ruled everyday life at the Puyallup Assembly Center where we were imprisoned. For example, there were twice-a-day roll calls. Parents had to instruct their children in all the rules and regulations of the prison camps, and the authorities expected the children to understand and obey these rules.

There seemed to be lines everywhere for everything— whether waiting for meals three times a day, using the toilet or a shower, or receiving items distributed by prison authorities. At first, the lines were long and slow moving, but the line problem eventually improved as the inmates made adjustments to better accommodate these lines.

At first, Puyallup had a "lights out" curfew, often signified with a bugle call that sounded throughout the acres of barracks. After lights out, armed guards in watchtowers manned searchlights that roamed the grounds throughout the night, leaving no doubt that the Japanese American civilians were now prisoners to be guarded and controlled within the barbed wire confines of the camps. It was nearly impossible to sleep soundly with the constant searchlights piercing the darkness, along with all the night noises.

My family had been torn apart that morning the FBI took Papa away. And now, my family was torn from our home in Seattle. Mama was doing her best to keep us together in a situation completely out of her control. The Japanese community norms were not always generous to single mothers in Mama's situation. I do not remember feeling any sorrow for Mama's challenges at the time because I was too young to understand anything beyond my own immediate reality. I was barely five years old. I do remember that after being in the prison camp for a while, I often wished I had my father. No doubt Mama needed him, too. The immense pressure would take a toll on Mama over the next couple of years, and she would age, grow weaker, and look sickly—but she *did* persevere and she *did* keep her family together.

Japanese call this kind of fortitude *gaman*—the ability to do one's best in distressed times and maintain self-control and discipline. Mama had *gaman*.

Papa, right, with his mother and brothers in Sendai, Japan.

CHAPTER 6

THE ANCESTORS, ROOTS OF STRENGTH

As an adult, I began to understand and appreciate my Japanese heritage—my family's *gaman* (perseverance)—and the roots of my parents' and grandparents' strengths to endure tremendous hardships and still rise to face a new day. Their strengths would become our inspiration to survive great hardships. There is a Japanese proverb that says, "Seven times I may fall. Eight times I will rise."

Those are the kind of people I came from—people with staunch resilience in difficult times. Once I understood the strengths—and frailties—of those that preceded me in my family, I began to appreciate what made it possible for my immediate family to survive four years of imprisonment in three different American concentration camps during World War II. Years later, I would understand that the strengths of the ancestors, passed down to us as if imbedded in our DNA, would keep my family together with dignity and hope for a better future.

Mama and Papa came to America separately and under very different circumstances, yet they both endured difficult times. They had notable differences in their backgrounds and personalities, yet they were married for 61 years until Papa's death in 1987. Because my father was originally from Sendai in northern Japan, and my mother was born in Hawaii and later raised on a remote island in southern Japan, it was unlikely my parents would have met but their life circumstances led them both to Washington State.

In so many ways my parents were opposites: Papa was overweight and Mama was a stick; Papa was gregarious, while Mama was shy. And perhaps most importantly, Mama thought herself to be a realist, while Papa was a perennial optimist. Contrasts between my parents were numerous, yet they married and found a way to forge a meaningful life together. In Japanese culture, to openly profess one's love for another was discouraged and considered improper and private. Still, their love for one another was strong, even though unspoken.

My parents had two major values in common. One was a love for children, and the other was a dislike of alcohol. If Papa even had just two or three sips of sake, his face turned bright red. He was allergic to alcohol, which turned out to be a good thing. Mama just never cared for alcohol, so it wasn't a problem.

Papa was named Masao Takahashi and was the second of four boys. He grew up in the busy city life of Sendai, the capital of Miyagi Prefecture. My father's surname, Takahashi, was a common name in the Sendai area, which was his *mother's* surname, or what we call her maiden name. Her full name was Kikuno Takahashi, and although I never met her I learned she was one strong-willed woman, defying her own cultural norms if need be. Her first marriage was terminated when she refused to return to her husband's household after the birth of their first child. Her problem was with the mother-in-law, someone Kikuno couldn't get along with, even though she got along with her husband. Kikuno's first husband often hung around her ancestral home, encouraging his wife to return to his family house. Both her husband's family and her family pressured Kikuno to return, but she refused. Her husband's family threatened, and then *demanded*, that at *least* the baby of their union be returned to the father's house.

I cannot imagine how a young woman in Japan during the late 1800s was able to withstand the pressure that my *obaachan* endured. In the end, she did concede their baby daughter to her husband's family, and she returned to the comfort of her original family. I do shake my head in amazement just thinking of my grandmother. And I am pleased that my *obaachan* was such a spunky woman.

When Kikuno felt ready to be a wife again, she decided to exercise the acceptable Japanese practice of bringing a husband to *her* family rather than joining *his* family. In this scenario, the new husband inherited the role as the head of the clan while giving up his original clan name. This practice was used on occasion in Japan with families that had no male heirs. The new male was identified as a "Yoshi."

Kikuno's second husband's full name was Katsusaburo Matsumoto before he became Yoshi of the Takahashi clan. Kikuno's surname, Takahashi, was given to her husband, their four sons (including my father), and to the sons' offspring. There was little question of Kikuno's enormous influence in family matters. She was certainly a feisty woman and many enjoyable stories about her antics flourished. She was considered the "power behind the throne," yet she rarely stayed "behind" the throne. Most people found her to be a social spark and a kindhearted woman with an adventurous soul, full of fun.

Katsusaburo could not match his wife in getting attention. She had a way of wrapping herself around anyone she met, while her husband barely got minimal polite support. As the head of the clan, he was expected to run the family business as a wholesaler for a wide range of products, mostly food-related. When the Japanese economy took a downturn, the family business suffered. There was also talk that my grandfather was not a strong manager, which contributed to his financial woes. He decided to leave Sendai for America where he hoped to reestablish himself in a profitable business. Kikuno stayed in Japan with their four sons.

For awhile, Katsusaburo lived in Canada where he managed to build a modestly successful dry cleaning business that he shared with one of his sons. In 1913, Masao was 19 years old when he traveled to America looking for his father. When he found him, he encouraged his father to return to Japan. It didn't take much in the way of persuasion because by then, Katsusaburo was sick and needed help. Sadly, a short time after he returned to Japan, he passed away. I never knew my *ojiisan* (grandfather).

Privately, Masao seemed to think of the trip to the United States as an adventure. As a young man, the opportunity to travel to America was full of excitement. He found the cultural differences between the two countries intriguing. For Masao, some of the abundant societal rules in Japan were excessive and a damper to enjoyment of life—even though he led a relatively happy, financially secure life with his family in Japan.

Masao was definitely his mother's son. Hearing stories of my father's youth—and actually meeting many of my relatives in Japan much later in my life— was quite exciting. According to my relatives, Papa was considered extraordinarily handsome in his youth. His good looks, charming personality, humor, genuine affection for people, and his generosity all came to him with ease. His attributes were a good counter balance to his mischievousness, his tendency to work around serious issues, a stubborn optimism, persistent procrastination and a general lack of attention to details.

For twenty years, Papa struggled to subsist in the United States working as a waiter, a logger, and a maintenance man. By the time I was born, my father had a job as a foreman for the Kodiak Fisheries Company. He enjoyed this job and felt fortunate to be paid so well as an immigrant worker. His job with Kodiak might have paid about $2,000 a year, considered a good wage at the time. Papa's job was to recruit workers for the summer trips to Alaska to work in a fish processing plant. The work was exhausting and demanding with crude accommodations and mediocre meals, but it paid well for temporary work. Parents of young college students routinely urged Papa to choose their sons for jobs at the fish company. High paying, short-term jobs were relatively difficult to find.

Finally, Papa had a good paying job, a great family with four healthy children, and high hopes of the Great Depression ending for good. Papa felt very fortunate and looked forward to a comfortable future. But his dream was not to be. Papa's job came to an abrupt end through no fault of his own. The happy and secure life with his family in Seattle came tumbling down, caught up in the consequences of a world at war.

In contrast to Papa, Mama's background was austere. Apparently, when Mama was born in Hawaii the midwife was quite sure she wouldn't survive for long and did not bother to register her birth. When a month and a half went by and the baby seemed to be winning the struggle for survival, the midwife decided to go ahead with the birth registration and my mother was named Hisako.

To avoid embarrassment or confusion, the midwife decided to ignore Hisako's actual date of birth on October 2, 1902 and replaced that date with her made up date of November 10, 1902. This is how Mama gained an extra birthday. Years later when Mama had her own children, we celebrated both her birthdays and Mama liked that.

I was told that by birthright, Mama should have been an American citizen because she was born in Hawaii, a U.S. territory since 1898. Her parents, Banjiro Suyetani and Yoshino Suyetani, were immigrants from Japan, so Mama legally could have had dual citizenship with Japan and Hawaii. However, anti-Asian sentiment in the United States led to laws that barred her parents from becoming U.S. citizens. Apparently, Mama was also a citizen of Japan by virtue of being the offspring of Japanese citizens. Years later while researching our family history, my siblings and I were unaware of Mama's right to dual citizenship, but we surmised she gave up her U.S. citizenship. There had been no recognition of Mama's U.S. citizenship in our family discussions or in any of the few documents that we had in our possession.

From birth, Hisako was treated as an "immigrant alien" by the U.S. government, and no one, including the family, seemed to think of her in any terms other than an *Issei*, a first-generation Japanese resident in the U.S. No doubt by cultural standards, Hisako was clearly *Issei*. She was definitely steeped in Japanese culture, language, history, and religion. Hisako was well acquainted with all the Japanese children's stories and fairy tales, and she was taught Japanese historical stories. Every morning she prayed in front of the family's small Shinto shrine. Hisako revered the Emperor and she took great pride in being Japanese.

For the first four years of her life, Hisako had been well-cared for in Hawaii. Her brother, Kiyoshi Suyetani, Uncle Roy to us kids, was two years older than his sister and they had a mutually valued bond that lasted throughout their lives. No sibling relationship could have been closer and sweeter than Hisako and her brother.

In 1906, the family dairy farm in Hawaii ended when the cows were put down due to hoof-and-mouth disease. Hisako and Kiyoshi returned to Japan with their mother, while their father went to San Francisco looking for farming opportunities. With a stroke of

Mama and her older brother,
Kiyoshi, in southern Japan.

amazing luck, he left San Francisco on April 16, 1906. Two days later, the infamous San Francisco earthquake struck and the city was devastated. It would have been a sorrowful overload for my grandfather to have to deal with the demise of his livelihood in Hawaii, shortly followed by San Francisco's major earthquake that may have taken his life. Instead, he had made arrangements to farm in Wapato in eastern Washington. How he got this job is a mystery to me. When he finally settled down, he made arrangements to have his wife and son, Kiyoshi, join him at his new farm in Washington. His daughter, Hisako, was left in Japan with relatives. The two closest people in my mother's life were suddenly whisked out of her life.

My mother's relatives in Japan turned cold toward her even though she was still a child. Her school friends began to avoid her as "a person without family." Years later, Mama recalled watching parents swinging their child between them while strolling down a road. She envied them and their togetherness as a family. As time passed, Hisako couldn't even remember what her father looked like. Her brother, who was her confidant and her protector, and her mother, who gave her emotional support, were gone.

In the end, my mother's sense of independence and personal strength would serve her well throughout her life. She also knew that her brother loved her, even though no words were exchanged. She simply knew her brother cared for her and this gave her great support throughout her life. Hisako finished her formal education requirements in Japan by finishing middle school and then eagerly awaited her parents' summons to America where she longed to be.

Finally, when Hisako was fifteen years old, her father made arrangements for her to come to America. She had spent her childhood away from her family, living in Japan for eleven years. In later years when talking about the family history, Mama never sounded happy about her relatives in Japan, but she also did not give us much of a clue as to what caused her unhappiness. It was clear that the independence she needed during that time basically made her stronger.

Hisako was so excited to do family things *together*. She looked forward to eating a meal for the first time with every family member at the table, including her new little brother, Shigemitsu Suyetani, who was born in Wapato, Washington. He was just a toddler barely walking when Hisako met him for the first time.

Mama's father, my *ojiichan*, was a hard working, serious, controlling, and stubborn man. He viewed the open expression of his emotions as a weakness. On the other hand, his wife, my *obaachan*, was sweet, gentle, and an openly loving person. She had a persistent, quiet strength—unlike my assertive paternal grandmother in Japan. For example, *Obaachan Suyetani* was a smoker, which was scandalous for Japanese women in her time. But that didn't stop *Obaachan;* she just calmly smiled and continued lighting up her next smoke.

By the time Hisako reached America, her beloved brother Kiyoshi was no longer living with the family. She learned that their father had thrown Kiyoshi out of the house after an argument. He had angrily denounced his son Kiyoshi as no longer a part of the family and announced that he was father to only *one* son—the toddler Shigemitsu. As a result, Hisako soon felt her presence in the household served as a betrayal to her brother Kiyoshi, whom she considered more devoted to her than her controlling father. Hisako's older brother was the one who supported her and she felt his brotherly love was indispensable.

Hisako's family reunion in Wapato turned into a short visit. Hisako's mother slipped some money to her daughter, who then made her way to Seattle to look for her brother. With little money, unable to speak English, unfamiliar with this new country, and knowing no one in Seattle other than her brother, Hisako made her way into the big city. I assume she was heartbroken, and probably angry, realizing her family life had fallen apart. I have often wondered, *Where did she find the boldness to strike out on her own under these circumstances, especially at fifteen years old?*

I now realize I come from tough women on both sides of the family!

When Hisako somehow reached the apartment where her brother lived, she learned he was in Alaska and would not return for many weeks. Luckily, the apartment owner was a kind woman and Hisako got permission to use the room until her brother returned from his trip to Alaska.

Her reunion with Kiyoshi was far different from the greeting she received from her parents, which was formal and subdued, yet delightfully interspersed with sweet and funny impishness from her new little brother, nicknamed Shigo. Hisako and Kiyoshi had a wonderful reunion. He gave Hisako a huge hug—yes, a *real* hug. That hug may have been the only hug *ever* between the two of them up to that point. Hugging was not part of the traditional Japanese culture, except on extreme occasions, such as their reunion after eleven years apart.

As a young woman, Hisako saw two options to become financially independent. One was to become a waitress and the other was to become a barber. The waitress jobs were available immediately but the barber job needed training and a license to practice. Hisako preferred the barber choice as more dignified. Fortunately, Kiyoshi helped her with the training costs. He was so proud of his sister when she officially became a barber.

It was Hisako's job as a barber that led her to meet the man she would marry. In Seattle's *Nikkei* community, the number of men far outnumbered the women so finding a man to marry was much easier than finding a woman to marry. Masao happened to be Kiyoshi's good friend. One day, Kiyoshi brought his friend Masao to the barbershop where he met Hisako.

Years later, we would ask about that fateful day. "Mama, Mama, were you nervous cutting his hair? Did your heart thump? Did you know immediately that this was the man you were going to marry?"

With a straight face she'd answer, "I cut his hair like I cut lots of hair. I do remember noticing he had very fine hair."

"Awww, Mama, aren't you going to even admit you noticed how good looking he was?"

Then she'd smile a little at the thought of their first meeting. Later, she mentioned she was mostly impressed that he was a nondrinker. That was all we could get her to admit about her first impressions of Papa. However, when we were older we determined that Papa had the looks, charm, and optimism, while Mama was blessed with a sizeable amount of inner fortitude. All of these attributes would serve them well.

After my parents married, they continued to stay close with Kiyoshi. Papa was aware of the ill feelings between Kiyoshi and his father, our *ojiichan*, although Papa had never met his father-in-law. Papa didn't feel right not acknowledging his in-laws who lived in the same state. Papa wanted to find a good way to end the estrangement. So, he kept urging Mama to reach out to her parents and make amends, especially since they now had grandchildren they had not met.

By this time, Mama's little brother, Shig, was grown and he was our Uncle Shig. He visited us regularly, driving his truck from Wapato to Seattle. When he returned home, he would share information with our *obaachan* about her grandchildren as well as her son Kiyoshi's life. Shig did not share family news with *Ojiichan*, a stubborn and prideful man who had not gotten past his anger. *Ojiichan* continued to act uninterested in his grown children's lives.

Finally, with Papa's ongoing encouragement, Mama relented and made her second trip out to Wapato, this time with her two daughters and husband in tow. *Obaachan* was overjoyed when she first saw her granddaughters. On the other hand, *Ojiichan* grimaced when he saw his daughter and her family, and then walked out into the field, not even acknowledging them. After a short interval, Papa followed after his father-in-law. *Obaachan* was preoccupied with the grandkids, but Mama watched her husband and her father converse in the distance. Papa worked his charm. Mama couldn't hear what they were saying, but it was obvious her father made a few short responses at first, but then continued talking with his son-in-law. Within a half hour, they walked back to the house together, laughing, in great humor as if they were close friends. From that point forward, our family made periodic visits to the farm and *both* of our grandparents greeted us with joy.

Obaachan was diagnosed with lung cancer several years later, and her husband allowed her to move into our Seattle home so she would be close to medical services. Our grandfather never visited us in Seattle. *Obaachan* lived with us until her death in 1941. Mama tried to console herself following her mother's death by noting that her mother didn't have to endure the hardships of World War II or incarceration in prison camps, which all unfolded several months after her death.

Obaachan's death had spared her the injustices, stress, and dehumanizing experience of life in Japanese American concentration camps.

CHAPTER 7

FROM BARRACKS TO HORSE STALLS

Life in the barracks involved many inconveniences. The barrack provided minimal protection from the weather. We suffered greatly in the stifling heat and stale humidity. Ventilation from the one window in each small living area was usually so poor that a candle would not even make a flicker with the window wide open in the sweltering heat. Many people were forced outside to look for shade anywhere they could. The stifling heat, along with the accumulation of dust and sand, made living conditions horrendous. The tarpaper did little to stop the dust and sand from entering the barracks. On occasion, the sand storms became so strong, it hurt exposed skin and stung our eyes.

For some three months, we endured the hot and humid summer in Puyallup. Then we began to worry about Washington's oncoming cold weather in the fall. For those families with vulnerable elderly members or young children, there were growing concerns for their health. The future was unknown and potentially deadly.

There was no running water in the barracks, so in the morning we had to first get dressed and then take our toothbrushes, toothpaste, toilet paper, and towels with us to the communal bathroom for our area that served twelve to fourteen barracks. With hundreds of people sharing one public bathroom, the lines could be long.

Every family was allotted a limited number of toilet paper rolls, depending on the size of the family. One evening, a problem occurred when seemingly everyone came down with diarrhea. People suspected the spoiled food served in the mess hall had made them sick. People scurried around, attempting to borrow the scarce tissue from neighbors. Apparently, the guards got suspicious when they noticed the unusually heavy, late night activity. They put the military guards on alert, suspecting a possible insurrection, and support personnel prepared to enter the compound to handle the "crisis." However, the guards soon realized the reason for the suspicious activity and canceled further interference. The inmates had an occasion to snicker, commenting that the searchlights were finally put to better use than irritating people trying to fall asleep.

If we needed to use the bathroom in the night, we had to change from pajamas to outdoor clothes, or put on a coat and walk to the latrine while the searchlight followed our trail. Once we were done, the guards kept the searchlight on us while we walked back to our barrack. Most adults found this disturbing and humiliating. As a child, I wondered if the guard with the searchlight was just trying to light the way for us. I'll never know, but I thought it was a possibility.

There was one young girl who had a different perspective on the searchlight following her to the latrine. For Peggy, it became an opportunity to use her imagination. Peggy was ten years old when she was first confined in the concentration camps. On her treks to the latrine, Peggy would imagine herself being honored as "Miss America" or some big time Hollywood celebrity. As the searchlight followed her, she would put on her biggest smile and wave to the imagined crowd of adoring fans. She pranced along the board pathway to the latrine, pausing now and then to point, wave, and wink at people in the imaginary crowd. Once she reached her destination, Peggy took a few quick curtsies before entering. And when she re-emerged, Peggy rewarded her imaginary fans with a huge smile and big waves of her arms. Then, Peggy added a few twirls and blew kisses to the crowd on her way back to her barrack.

Years later, Peggy told a group of us listening to her story that she thoroughly enjoyed those moments in the "limelight." I lived in a fantasy world much of my childhood days in the camps, so I love thinking of Peggy taking that long celebrity walk to and from the latrine. I do wonder what the guards who followed Peggy's antics with the searchlight may have thought. In her own childhood world, Peggy found a way to rise above the humiliation and oppression of guards watching her every move to the latrine.

In recent years, my friend May Namba, told me that every time she sees a "replica" of a barrack's room in a photo, a museum, or a historical display, she says, "The real barrack room I remember wasn't nearly as nice as this." The barren atmosphere of the camps most likely can never be accurately duplicated.

Mrs. Hayashida was among the Bainbridge Island residents who were the first to be forced from their homes in 1942. There is a famous photo of her carrying her baby while boarding the ferry on her way to the concentration camp. Over six decades later in 2007, Mrs. Hayashida joined the annual Pilgrimage to Minidoka at 96 years old. Upon visiting the refurbished barrack, she said the same thing as May Namba. "The real barrack room I remember wasn't nearly as nice as this."

Someone laughingly added, "This is a *deluxe* version of what the living space in the barracks really looked like."

With no running water in the barracks, women had to do the family laundry in a designated room with a row of sinks. Quickly, the laundry room also became a place where women had the opportunity to share information and socialize. For hours, they would scrub and rinse and wring out their clothes, all by hand on scrubboards, often until their hands were red and raw. Then, they'd hang them on clotheslines to dry. A new mother at that time, Shigeko Uno, recalled waking up early on cold mornings to stand in line waiting for the laundry room to open. She brought her scrubboard, bucket, soap and a pile of dirty diapers. The early birds got the hot water, so women wanted to be among the first to secure an available sink and hot water. Shigeko had a neighbor in the camp who was a mother of ten kids, which Shigeko thought was unbelievable. She often wondered how this mother was able to cope with all the laundry needs of her large family.

PHOTO: MOHAI, SEATTLE POST-INTELLIGENCER COLLECTION

A woman washing clothes at
Puyallup Camp

After several weeks or more at Puyallup, the camp authorities told our family that we were to be transferred out of area "A" (the parking lot) to area "D." I don't recall how long we were placed in the original barracks, but I do remember we were there long enough that my family was thrilled to be moving out. We had high hopes for improved living in area "D," which was within the fairground proper. This move was prompted because our youngest sister, Midori, had come down with the measles, so our family had to move into an "isolation ward." We anticipated this move would surely be an upgrade because of Midori's illness.

As we packed up our belongings, Mama cautioned us to not appear too enthusiastic about leaving. She was concerned about hurting the feelings of neighbors

PHOTO: MOHAI, SEATTLE POST-INTELLIGENCER COLLECTION

Muddy streets of "Camp Harmony" at Puyallup.

we were leaving behind. She also worried about the illnesses we would encounter in an isolation ward, especially tuberculosis (TB). At that time, TB was the most dreaded of diseases. We said hurried good-byes to a few friends and rushed out of area "A." To reach area "D" we needed to first cross the gate out of area "A", then cross a rather busy street in Puyallup, then re-enter into another gate to get to area "D." Although two soldiers escorted our family, my sisters commented that we had a brief taste of freedom while crossing the street. We laughed.

Our high hopes for improved living quarters were soon dashed. We were totally unprepared, actually horrified, for what confronted us when we were shown our new quarters. The isolation ward was, in fact, the horse stables on the fairgrounds. "They can't really mean for us to live in the horse stall could they?" my sister Kazu mumbled. "It's really stinky in here. Do they really think we're horses?"

Mama stood silent, staring for a few moments. Then, without a word, she picked up a broom and started sweeping up some hay left in the area by the former occupants. She proceeded to wash down the walls, and we helped her scrub, but nothing reduced the powerful, awful smell of horses and manure. We had complained a lot about living in the regular barracks, but very quickly that began looking good once we arrived at the horse stalls. Before long, we learned to take the Fels-Naptha soap and cut off little chips to mask the stench. This soap did not have a very nice odor, but it was definitely a stronger odor than the horse stable. We tied a handkerchief over the soap chips and put this under our noses when we were trying to fall asleep. We swore it helped mask the horse smell and helped us fall asleep. At the time, we thought we were quite clever learning this trick.

CHAPTER 8

A PROPHECY
IN THE MEDICAL WARD?

The assembly centers were crowded with people living in unsanitary conditions. This posed serious health threats to many, so those who got sick were sent to the isolation ward in the horse stalls, away from the main population.

I cannot begin to imagine the misery the adults experienced in this isolation ward, but for me as a child, this move was somewhat of a challenging adventure. It was like a scene from a movie. Never before had I seen so many people moaning in bed. I wondered if a few of them were still alive; they looked pale and motionless. One woman seemed to always be quietly crying. A few others had gauze bandages wrapped around different parts of their bodies. Some looked fine, and I didn't understand why they were in this medical ward. Maybe they were like me, accompanying a sick family member to the isolation ward.

Every once in awhile we heard arguments, but arguments among the adults at the camp seemed normal. I spent a lot of time just "people watching," fascinated by all the people and new activities in this strange place. I made up stories about some of the people in my fantasy world, but I never talked to anyone outside of my family. I knew at an early age not to be seen as "nosy," or intrude on other people—but it was okay to let my imagination go wild.

I remember the divided doors to the horse stalls; separated into top and bottom parts, each opening independently. Living under these circumstances would seem bizarre and unreal to most, but as a child these conditions quickly became a part of everyday life. While living in the smelly horse stalls, we spent even less time in our assigned area and more time outside in the fresh air.

I suspect it was more than the smell that disturbed the adults. They were humiliated, demeaned, and distressed to be forced to live in such undignified and subhuman conditions. How do people keep their dignity when they are being treated as animals? Years later I would understand what that meant, and think about it often.

As I look back, I am more disturbed today about the horse stalls being used to house us than I was at the time. Today, I am pained thinking about those living conditions for Japanese Americans in the prison camps. In many ways, it was a blessing to be an ignorant child. In my old age, it seems so silly to cry over what occurred so many years ago, but I still cry. My dignity was not at stake as a child imprisoned at Puyallup, but as an adult, my dignity is still at stake.

The one thing I clearly remember from the "horse stall" days is a woman's loud voice persistently calling out the same Japanese words over and over again throughout the night. Her repetitious calling was a nightly occurrence and must have disturbed others in the isolation ward. I was curious about this woman but I didn't necessarily feel bad for her. At that time, I knew nothing of adults being mentally tormented by their own demons, or that this woman's nightly cries of anguish might be causing embarrassment to her family. In those days, exhibiting emotional distress was too often judged as indicative of character weakness and dishonor. What worse place could there be for a family seeking privacy than in this isolation ward in a crowded concentration camp?

I was oblivious to all these concerns. Older kids tried to scare us little ones by telling us that this woman disliked young children. The bigger kids would tell us little kids, "She could go mad and she might chop you up while you sleep."

Even though I was only five, I knew they were making up these stories. I felt smug and too "big" to believe this nonsense. However, all the same, I did try to stay up as long as I could at night, just in case. And sometimes, I was surprised when I woke up in the morning, still alive! It is only because of the scary stories about her that I remember this woman at all. The adults were experiencing unspeakable heartache and anguish, so maybe the kids were just inventing their own terror ideas of disaster. Mostly, the children were protected from the adult woes in the concentration camps, but the children did not escape *feeling* the tensions that surrounded them.

Decades later, my sister and I were talking about "camp days'" when one of us mentioned the woman who called out nightly. I admitted I had completely forgotten what it was the woman was saying, but my sister remembered her exact words. *"Nakagawa kocho sensei Nihon ne kaese."* That translated to "Return Principal Nakagawa back to Japan."

How could I have forgotten the words the woman repeated night after night? But forget, I did. When my sister told me, I got goose bumps. "How strange is that?" I asked my sister.

My family name was not Nakagawa but Takahashi. Yet, some fifteen years later, I married a man with the last name Nakagawa and he would become a school principal. In addition, I also would become a school principal. I became *Nakagawa kocho sensei* (Principal Nakagawa). With that realization, I could hear the "Twilight Zone" theme song in the recesses of my memory. It was strange and scary.

I ruminated over this for quite some time. *Did that woman program my future? Was it a prophecy?*

Finally, I decided that whatever influence she may have had on me, I sure could have done a lot worse than becoming Principal Nakagawa. Perhaps I should give belated thanks to the woman whose name I do not even know. I did learn that she was the mother of a woman I knew. She had worked at the Japanese Language School and for some reason took issue with the principal of the school. The family seemed unaware of what the problem was. I was pleased to learn that eventually she did overcome her mental distress.

When I learned more about this woman and her circumstances, I did feel a tinge of guilt about the kids making up stories at her expense. In those days, mental illness was often thought of as a character weakness, and as kids, we didn't know any better. In my adult years, I did feel remorse for having possibly added to the woes of the family with our childish behavior. Eventually, I wrote a story using her as the central heroic figure to make up for our folly.

And the final piece to the mystery about this woman —when I was an adult and traveled to Japan for the first time, it did flash in my mind that I was fulfilling this woman's prophecy: Principal Nakagawa went back to Japan!

CHAPTER 9

Strange Benjo

The communal bathroom was quite a contraption and an improvement over the smelly outhouses. A big bucket sat high off the floor with water running into it. When it became heavy enough to outweigh the counter balance, the bucket came crashing down. On its downward fall, the bucket would get tripped. That was when the spectacle began.

Gushing water would fill the trough running under the length of a long bench with a half-dozen holes on top. These holes were designed for people to sit on when going to the bathroom. This was the first and only toilet I have ever seen that flushed horizontally. At regular intervals, roaring water rushed through the trough and picked up human waste. To avoid the spray caused by the force of the water, anyone using the first hole on the bench, closest to the bucket, had to time her use to intervals between flushes. To a five year old, this seemed like a wondrous adventure, especially when the gushing water roared down the trough.

Privacy did not exist in the latrines in the camps. There were no partitions anywhere. Each user, including those waiting for their turn, had full view of everyone else. It was only the urgent need to go to the bathroom that overcame any need for modesty. Some women even brought cardboard boxes that they held in front of themselves while using the latrine to have some modicum of privacy and dignity.

As an adult, I learned this set up in the latrine was one more way these prisons dehumanized us and took away our dignity. However, as a child, I was unaffected. Mostly, I was entranced with how it all worked. Early on, Mama taught me "bathroom etiquette" befitting the circumstances. She taught me that while sitting on the row of toilets, avoid eye contact with others, and don't say "Hi" to people I knew.

One time when I was using the *benjo*, some older girls were giggling about *obasaans* (grandmothers) who would often wipe themselves by leaning forward and reach between their legs. Their movements were slower and more awkward, so the girls laughed, perhaps embarrassed to witness such private bathroom habits.

I must admit that I laughed at the breach of manners as well as at the mental picture. I, too, was guilty of breaking the code from time to time with surreptitious glances. But I did something much worse. My curiosity drove me to actually look into the hole while the water was gushing past. I was shocked to see toilet tissue soaked with blood passing by. Only one young woman was sitting to my right. I recognized her as the beautiful lady who was always nice—even to us little kids. I thought, *How sad that she is dying of some terrible disease that's making her bleed so much.*

My heart was pounding at the sight of this nice lady's bloody toilet paper, and tears began to form in my eyes. Quietly, I followed this nice lady after we left the *benjo*. I was worried about her. I could not believe her upbeat attitude, acting as if nothing was wrong! Secretly, I watched her smile and talk with people cheerfully. I thought, *I could never be able to do that if I was dying like her!*

I tried to keep that nice lady's secret, but finally, I blurted it out to my best friend who was a year older than me. When my friend found out *how* I learned of this tragedy, she broke out in peals of laughter. She called me "naive," a word I had never heard before. She explained blood on toilet paper was *not* a sign of death. Then my friend took a deep breath and went on to say it was simply the result of a person eating too many beets. From that day forward, I never ate beets again. It was not much of a sacrifice—I never liked beets anyway!

CHAPTER 10

$\mathcal{S}$WEET $\mathcal{C}$ONNECTIONS

One hot day in Puyallup as my family was settling into the boredom of camp life something unusual and unforgettable happened. I followed my sister Kazu to the fence line just across the street from a small grocery store located outside of the camp.

From time to time, Kazu would go to this special place by the fence where, on the other side, white kids walked by on their way home from school. The Puyallup Assembly Center was located on the fairgrounds in the middle of the City of Puyallup. The camp had separate areas cut off from one another by city streets. This resulted in a bizarre, cruel juxtaposition of white kids walking down the streets on their way home, living in freedom and looking at fenced-in Japanese kids who longed to simply walk across the street and get an ice cream.

Sometimes, the white kids were willing to take coins from the kids in the camp. That day, Kazu held out her coins through the fence and a boy took the money. He ran across the street to the store to buy ice cream for my sister and other kids inside of the fence.

This was a frequent exchange among the kids. No one questioned the honesty of the ice cream runners. They could have easily run off with our money and there was no way we could have chased them. But most didn't and they didn't expect to be paid for their ice cream delivery service.

I have often wondered, *What went through my sister's mind as she watched the white kids run freely across the street to buy ice cream when she couldn't?*

To this day, whenever I reflect on this, I still ask myself, *What motivated the kids to run that errand?* In turn, I think, *What did the white kids think seeing kids their own age as prisoners behind the barbed-wire fences? Did the kids on each side ever talk about anything besides getting ice cream?*

The adults erected the fences. The children, in their own small way, found how to breach the barrier that divided them.

The ice cream on that hot day was delicious.

More than 40 years later in the 1980s, I was speaking on a social justice panel in Washington, D.C. I mentioned my childhood incarceration but did not include the ice cream story. Afterward, a group of people approached the panel participants to ask more questions and share stories. Among them stood a lone white man patiently waiting to speak to me in private.

Once we had time to talk, the man vividly recalled his mother being very upset that Japanese Americans were being incarcerated for no reason other than their race. She had passionately expressed her opposition to the injustice of this action the government took. "It's against the very principles of American democracy!" she had declared to her family.

The man told me he had his mother's anger in mind when, as a young boy, he walked past the Puyallup Assembly Center with some friends. He was particularly dismayed to see so many imprisoned children. After that, he made it a practice to buy ice cream for the Japanese American kids behind the fence. He also mentioned that when his family moved from Puyallup to New York City, his mother arranged to sponsor two Japanese American students so they could leave the concentration camp and continue their education. Once the two students arrived at their home to live with them, his mother emphatically told him he was to treat them respectfully.

I knew about people who sponsored Japanese American students, but this was the first time I had heard from anyone who had been on the other side of the fence in Puyallup getting ice cream for the imprisoned kids. Suddenly, I felt strongly connected to this man. He may have been the exact same person who had brought Kazu and me that delicious ice cream so many years ago. I thought, *Sweet man—sweet ice cream.*

I hugged him excitedly in gratitude and asked him to thank his mother for being such a beautiful person. He agreed, she was indeed a beautiful person. Then he promised to convey my thanks to her—in his prayers.

CHAPTER 11

SECOND PRISON CAMP, MINIDOKA

We left the Puyallup Assembly Center on Sept 2, 1942. The authorities told us to pack up because we were moving to a permanent camp at an undisclosed location. Even if the guards had told us where we were going, I suspect stating the destination as Minidoka, Hunt, or Twin Falls wouldn't have meant much to the prisoners. Many adults wondered how the "permanent" camp would differ from the "temporary assembly center." Once again, we faced a huge unknown that was beyond our control.

My little sister Midori had recovered from the measles, and we were all basically healthy by the time we had to move to the next unknown destination. My family was relieved to be getting out of the stinking horse stalls that served as a medical ward.

We were among the last people to leave Puyallup, along with Mrs. Matsudaira, who would be one of the final two inmates left at Puyallup. She and her family were close friends with our family. Her husband and my father both worked for the same Alaskan Kodiak Fishing Company. Mrs. Matsudaira and one other woman were pregnant and very close to delivery, so they were held back. Mrs. Matsudaira's husband and their nine children had already been transferred to the Minidoka prison camp.

The medical staff gave Mrs. Matsudaira two little white tablets she didn't recognize along with castor oil every morning to induce labor. After three days of this treatment and no sign of beginning labor, there was talk of putting the two pregnant women on the train. Mrs. Matsudaira feared going into labor while on the train, so she tried taking alternating hot and cold showers and even tried to induce labor by running hard for three blocks. On the evening of the third day, Mrs. Matsudaira's baby girl was finally born. The following morning, mother and newborn were boarded on the train by a stretcher passed through the train's window. Mrs. Matsudaira was just relieved she didn't have to endure labor and delivery on a moving train.

Our earlier departure from Puyallup was much less dramatic. My family was put on a bus with other *Nikkei* families and then loaded on a dilapidated train that appeared to have been pressed back into service to deliver us to our next destination. The train was filthy and the windows caked with mud and dust. The seats were worn thin or torn from too much use and neglect. Bathroom facilities were barely functional. Even as a little girl, I remember feeling uncomfortable because I constantly felt dirty at the camp with no relief in sight. Everything felt grimy.

Kazu had a friend who was excited about taking her first train ride. She wore her pretty white dress for this occasion. But in spite of her best efforts, it was impossible to keep her dress from becoming soiled in quick order on the grimy train. Kazu remembers being fascinated by the tumbleweeds she saw for the first time while staring out the train windows. She also recalls eating paper bag lunches passed out by the authorities. The dirt and dust did not interfere with her enjoyment of the food; in fact, Kazu was pleasantly surprised that the sandwiches tasted good. She drank her water allotment and wished she had more; the dust made her very thirsty.

Armed guards took their posts at each of the train's cars and discouraged people from getting up from their seats. Some of the riders played card games while others tried to nap. Finding distractions for the young kids took patience and imagination. Many people described the long trip to Minidoka in south central Idaho as tedious, monotonous, and very uncomfortable. The train made numerous stops, many of them in the middle of nowhere. No one had any idea why we were stopped. The guards insisted we pull down the blinds whenever there was any sign of civilization and sternly admonished anyone who peeked out, even a child. We never understood why the guards were so strict about lowering the blinds, and none of the guards ever bothered to explain it to us. Some people thought it was to keep us prisoners from knowing where we were going. Others thought the "blinds down" command was to prevent the public from seeing us or perhaps to prevent any unfortunate contact between the prisoners and the free citizens. Maybe it was just to be oppressive.

After a long and slow train ride more than 600 miles long, we arrived at the Minidoka prison camp, or as the WRA preferred to say, "relocation camps." No matter how creative our government got using euphemisms to soften our reality, this was another prison camp complete with barbed-wire fencing that faced inward and guard towers with armed military, machine guns, and searchlights.

Minidoka was one of ten major camps built by the U.S. military and administered by the government's War Relocation Authority (WRA). An arm of the civilian government administered these large camps, while the guards were part of the U.S. military. At its peak, the inmate population at Minidoka numbered 9,397 people. As late arrivals, we were assigned block number 36. My older sisters made sure I knew my new address: Block 36, Barrack 5, Space D, or "36-5-D." It was easy to get confused, especially as a child, because there were about 40 barracks and they all looked exactly the same. So I memorized "36-5-D" so I could get back to my family in case I got lost. As fourth in line in my family at the camp, I was assigned the letter "D." Papa was not included in this count.

Our arrival at Minidoka looked similar to our arrival at Puyallup—camp construction was far from complete and there was mud everywhere. The mud at Minidoka was extensive and deep, which made coping quite a challenge, especially at the beginning of our stay.

We were forced to use outhouses again. The sewer system was not yet completed and the recent rains had been persistent and strong. Kazu was particularly fearful of the mud compromising the stability of the ground under the outhouses. It was easy to see where the outhouse walls were crumbling under the steady rain. Years later, I read an account where a toddler had actually slipped into the muck and mud in one of the camps and drowned. Learning about details such as this saddens me to this day.

We waited a long time before we had flushing toilets at Minidoka. When the toilets became available, they were typical Western toilets, and unfortunately from my child's perspective, not the unusually interesting *benjos* at Puyallup that fascinated me. I'm sure the adults saw this much differently, but adults and children alike were grateful to not use outhouses anymore. The facilities still lacked partitions, so our dignity and privacy were once again challenged.

Later, when the mud dried up, it hardened into ruts left from tire tracks. In winter, the snow and ice hazards confronted us, and then in spring, we faced the deep thick mud once again. I remember the first time I saw icicles hanging from the barracks. I was fascinated, and I thought the icicles were extraordinarily beautiful.

One advantage of the onset of cold weather was the dramatic decrease of foul odors from the outhouses because the waste froze. The downside of cold weather was the limited supply of coal to fuel the potbelly stove in our small living space. Sufficient warmth was a constant concern. Without insulation in the barracks, it was impossible to maintain comfortable temperatures. On the plus side, the barrack rooms at Minidoka were an improvement over the barracks and horse stalls at Puyallup. At Minidoka, the walls were more substantial and more importantly, these walls reached the ceiling. Yes, we had a real ceiling and that reduced the sound traveling through the rafters. That small improvement offered people much more comfort.

By the time we settled into our new living quarters at Minidoka, baby Midori was allocated her own cot. She was still pinned between adjacent cots to prevent her falling to the floor, but her separate cot made sleeping a bit more comfortable. We had the cots, one light bulb, and a potbelly stove in our living area. There were no tables, chairs, closets, dressers, or desks.

The imprisoned families were getting clever in utilizing leftover lumber from the building work at the camp. The construction crew did not concern itself with cleaning up the leftovers. Finding lumber became a popular past time in the evening hours after the construction laborers closed down for the day. I understand the workers assigned men to watch over the lumber supply in the evening hours, however, as time went by, it was rumored that these same men charged with protecting the lumber, in reality assisted the inmates to secure the lumber they needed. Apparently, there were compassionate construction workers who ignored company rules and participated in helping the inmates while the bosses seemed to look the other way. Over time, there seemed to be an increase in chairs, desks, tables, and shelves appearing in the schools and in the barracks. Some rules were made to be broken. Despite the difficult situation, there were kind hearts who helped out in small ways.

At Minidoka I was enrolled in a makeshift school's kindergarten. Surprisingly, I enjoyed school. The teachers were not scary, partly because they didn't wear "habits" like the nuns at my older sisters' school in

Seattle. The fellow students were not as rowdy as I remember the students during my visits to the Seattle kindergarten. I did learn the Pledge of Allegiance in school, and I worked hard to pronounce "allegiance" and the word "indivisible" correctly, although I had no idea what those big words meant! Actually, I had no idea what the Pledge was all about, yet I was proud to recite the Pledge by rote and pronounce the terms almost correctly. It was only much later that I understood the irony of this pledge, placing my hand over my heart and saying the words, "...with liberty and justice for all" while I was a five-year-old kid made a prisoner behind the barbed wire fences of an American concentration camp.

Years later, as I began to understand the full gravity of my situation, I often asked myself, *Where was my liberty? Where was my justice?*

While I was in Minidoka, I started taking Japanese classical dancing. Kazu was becoming an accomplished dancer while she was still in Seattle, and I wanted to do what my big sister did. The dance teacher lived in the barrack next to ours, so it was convenient for us to take lessons. Our sister Nobu was not interested, but Kazu and I enjoyed the lessons and the subsequent recitals. I knew Kazu was a particularly talented dancer and I thought she was so beautiful. In time, I believed that I was a very good dancer, too, for my age. I hoped with enough practice, I would be as good a dancer as my big sister.

I must admit that I was not aware of the many burdens Mama endured. Only vaguely do I recall one incident in the laundry room when I saw Mama's stress: I was trying to pull Mama out of her conversation with

PHOTO: NAKAGAWA PRIVATE COLLECTION

Mako (second row, second from right)
with her kindergarten class in Minidoka.

another woman and bring her back to our living quarters so I could show her a new move I learned in my Japanese dancing class. I didn't see Mama's face full of anger, disbelief, and disgust until we were back in our room. I had never seen Mama so outraged; under normal circumstances she was calm and steady. Indeed, I wanted to hear what Mama was upset about. She breathed so hard and appeared so anguished. She did not cry. Instead, she calmed herself down and asked in Japanese how my dancing was coming along. Mama did not share her story of outrage, but instead protected me and focused on my dance moves. Maybe it's a good thing I didn't learn what caused Mama such anguish. Maybe it was an early lesson in learning to overcome my own outrage in later life.

Nobu joined the Girl Scouts. She enjoyed the craft activities and was full of energy. She seemed to be curious about everything and she especially enjoyed the outdoors. Nobu loved to tease Kazu and me about needing the white-face makeup for our recitals, something she didn't need for Girl Scouts. Mama encouraged each daughter to pursue activities of her choice. Even within the confines of the prison camp, Mama found outlets for us to be children.

Kazu was too young to be invited to the dances held by the older teenagers in the mess halls at the camps, which was probably a good thing. During World War II, the Swing, the Jitterbug, and the Jive were popular dances for young people. Kazu often pretended a handsome young man was dancing to some romantic tune and sweeping her off her feet. However, dancing was one activity Mama strongly opposed. She considered it obscene for a girl and a boy, who maybe didn't even know one another, to slap themselves against each other and move around the dance floor connected while moving to suggestive and provocative music. Mama thought this activity was just "asking for trouble" and basically, this type of dancing was immoral in her judgment.

I heard one mother who agreed with Mama, denouncing dancing as fit for immoral women who would eventually sell their bodies. I believe she was the same woman who marched into a dance session that her daughter secretly attended and bodily dragged her out of this intolerable situation. This incident was the talk of the rumor-mongering women in the camp. The breach between the adults and the young people had fertile grounds to fester at the camps and these dances created a significant wedge between the generations.

In general, everyone forced into these prison camps seemed bitter. People were bitter over different things, and angry people took out their frustrations on those closest to them. Over time, this bitterness and anger would continue to grow as thousands of us were forced into this crowded world not of our choosing.

CHAPTER 12

Mess Hall Culture

We all knew Mama didn't like the mess hall scene at all. "To begin with, you always feel you are part of a herd," she said. "I don't like being shuffled around like an animal. The noise is so loud and constant. I feel like I'm constantly looking for a handout, waiting in those long lines. It's simply undignified."

"Okay, okay Mama. You don't like the mess hall." We all understood!

Mama's complaints were not much different from other camp inmates, but I had the feeling that there was more to Mama's complaints than she was telling us. Day after day, we waited in long lines for breakfast, then again for lunch, then again for dinner. The routine never changed. Throughout the sweltering hot summer, the freezing cold of winter snowstorms, the rain, and the wind that stirred up frequent dust storms, we waited and waited.

Sometimes the mess hall food was pretty good but too many times the food was bad—especially eating things like mutton stew, liver, and beef tongue, which were not familiar to many in the Japanese culture. Many people were turned off by just the *thought* of this food, or maybe it was the smell, the texture, or its appearance. But with Vienna sausages it was a different story. Initially, we enjoyed this canned meat but grew to despise it. The turn off came when we were served Vienna sausages for breakfast, then again for lunch, and then again for dinner. Incredibly, this went on for many consecutive days—Vienna sausage for breakfast, lunch, and dinner. The Vienna sausage run would repeat over the ensuing months and it eventually sickened all of us. To this day, some 70 years later, some friends tell me they still feel nauseous even looking at a Vienna sausage.

The hard tack biscuits passed out to kids as a treat were renamed "dog biscuits" by the kids themselves. Although these odd biscuits were generously available, we usually avoided them. There was talk of spoiled food from time to time and many people simultaneously came down with diarrhea. Kazu loved fish from the time she was a little girl, before the camps. She eagerly anticipated a meal of Columbia smelt on Minidoka's dinner menu but couldn't believe how horrible it tasted. That was the first time she rejected a fish dinner. More than 70 years later, Kazu still loves fish, and loves smelt, but she still won't touch Columbia smelt. Another friend refuses to eat any fish ever since his time in the camps.

There never seemed to be enough food for the young people. Others left the mess hall still hungry because they could not stomach the substandard quality of the food. Often, food was the topic of conversation among the adults. There was talk about good food too, especially the food people longed for—sashimi, tempura, pickled

Japanese delicacies—but it was the conversations about "bad food" that were more interesting and dramatic.

The quality of the mess hall food was largely dependent on the skill of the head cook of each camp block. It didn't take long for word to get around that the food "in block such and such" was much better than other blocks. The lines for the mess halls with good cooks grew longer each day as people confirmed these rumors and passed on the information. The disproportionate number of people eating at the popular mess halls eventually became a problem. Soon, buttons were passed out to block residents to identify them as legitimate diners of that particular block. This brought the lines back to normal with a lot of disgruntled inmates. I'm sure some of the early eaters shared their identifying buttons with their friends.

All the cooks and helpers in the mess halls were inmates. We all pretty much understood that they were doing the best they could with what supplies the WRA distributed. I think the inclusion of beef tongue for dinner was the most surprising and distasteful dish served while we were at Minidoka—even worse than the Vienna sausage. Very few of the inmates knew that beef tongue was actually consumed and enjoyed by a number of people. For us, eating beef tongue appeared to be just as dehumanizing as living in horse stalls.

The cooks didn't know what to make of this new menu entrée and some inmates laughed while others cried. Many people just threw away the beef tongue dish and others complained loudly to the mess hall cooks. Beef tongue did cause a commotion, with most believing this was not fit for human consumption and an insult.

A common question for those waiting in line for dinner would be to ask those leaving the mess hall, "Was it a 'yuck,' or is it edible?"

On the "yuck" days, the canteen at Minidoka did a brisk business. It was stocked with convenience items, including a meager supply of snack food that inmates could purchase with their own money. Before long, a number of people decided to grow their own vegetables and prepare their own *tsukemono* (a side dish of salted vegetables), along with other foods they cooked themselves to complement their meals. Japanese farmers in the camps began planting and growing bountiful gardens filled with a wide assortment of vegetables. They grew zucchini, carrots, onions, squash, cucumbers, peas, radishes, lettuce, cabbage, potatoes, broccoli, eggplant, corn, tomatoes, watermelon, celery, peppers, turnips, and beans. With this bounty, there was no shortage of people to help the excellent farmers grow enough vegetables on large plots, some as large as 70 acres. The resourcefulness in the Japanese American community saved people from the mess halls' gastrointestinal disasters.

Families came up with creative ideas to make their meals more inviting. The electricity going to the one light bulb in each living unit served as an electrical source for unauthorized hot plates. My friend Janet

Baba's grandmother used to make a special sweet treat to share with her grandchildren. The family saved up for the occasion when Janet's mom, May Sakamoto, could make a full Japanese dinner for the family. That was certainly a welcome treat for the Sakamoto family in the midst of their imprisonment.

From time to time, fires erupted in the barracks. I wonder if overloaded electrical wires caused many of the fires. The big pot-bellied stoves also could have been the cause. Aside from providing heat for the room, the stove was often used to keep water hot for tea.

One white woman who visited the Minidoka camp remarked how nice it must be for the women in the camps to be relieved of the tiresome chore of cooking daily. Outsiders' misconceptions of the camps' mess halls as being positive and a "break" for women having to cook every day was part of the WRA's propaganda to justify this massive injustice. Many on the outside thought incarceration was a welcomed break from the tedious chores of daily life. There is no doubt that the women in camp would have gladly chosen to prepare individual meals for their own families in their own homes.

The need for more "family time" was becoming apparent, and the incarcerated families were blaming the mess hall operation as one of the major factors dividing families. Camp residents attested to the enormous cost to family relationships when the family did not gather to eat together. The essence of "family" began to crumble and blur. Camp eating arrangements, together with the cramped and Spartan barracks quarters, led children to spend less and less time with their families. Some young people only showed up at their "living areas" to sleep.

"Unruly children and young people" was the topic of much discussion among adults in camp, especially the *Isseis* who were accustomed to traditional family gatherings. Other than food, the mess halls served up hefty portions of news, gossip, complaints, rumors, arguments, and discussions on a wide range of topics. The majority of people tended to share meals with those who shared common interests. Most kids ate with their friends and enjoyed it, choosing to separate themselves from the family and older generations. Families where the parents insisted the children eat with them were rather unusual, or the children were still young.

The Japanese culture relies on strong family interaction during meals to cement their bonds and cultural values. Left more to their own devices, young teenagers began to display unruly behavior, unusual for *Nisei* youth prior to the camps. The young people enjoyed the diminished control from older family members and the increasing disrespect and arrogance of the youth troubled the adults. "Proper behavior" was going out the window, lamented the older generations. The traditional roles in a family, although sometimes amounting to stereotypical activities, became unclear and it was difficult to guide the young people. There was some evidence of gang-type activities developing. Many people felt the disruption of the family unit, and the diminishing influence of the parents and other adult role models. There was a concerted effort to provide activities for the young in more wholesome endeavors, but the problems of "youth rebellion" grew.

At the mess hall, I was able to escape the watchful eye of Mama who insisted I eat my vegetables. I hated vegetables then, and to this day, I am not big on vegetables. Even though I was only five, I often ate with friends or with my sisters who were not as insistent as Mama about vegetables. My friend and I used to laugh and chant, "Vegetables are for rabbits." We thought this was great fun, and in our own young and naïve way, we were being rebellious.

Mama often fell ill and my sisters brought food back to the barracks for her. Mama's spirit was always stronger than her frail body. It was not unusual for her to be suffering from a physical ailment. However, I suspect Mama wanted to limit her time with the mess hall crowd. We had been forced to become a family without a papa, and the Japanese culture did not always look kindly on single women with families. Mama's reluctance to eat in the mess hall may have been her discomfort in a large social setting. She was a private, and often, a shy person. Perhaps she wanted to avoid blatant stares and mean comments.

I will never know.

CHAPTER 13

THE BEST & WORST OF MANKIND

Wood planks had been placed over the deep mud leading to the outhouses at Minidoka. I am not sure why I stepped off of them and into the deep muck. Maybe the mud was making the planks slippery. Maybe I wanted to try out my "new" hand-me-down boots. Maybe, I just felt adventuresome.

Walking directly in the mud seemed all right for the first half dozen steps. Actually, it was kind of fun. Then, the squishy mud reached my ankles. My boots protected my shoes, but I couldn't lift my leg out of the thick mud for the next step. I leaned forward and grabbed the top of the right boot to pull my leg free. I could pick up my legs one at a time and inch forward, but it was a struggle to keep my coat from dragging through the mud. Lifting my coat, as well as one leg at a time was quite a balancing act for a five year old. Progress was slow, and to make matters worse, I urgently needed to get to the outhouse.

Often, I delayed using the latrines because other kids had told me that snakes sometimes hid in the holes, waiting to attack people. Mama told me that was nonsense but I was not completely convinced. Besides the possibility of snakes attacking me while I went to the bathroom, the smell alone was enough to keep me away as long as possible.

But now I was in trouble and the mud seemed to be getting deeper. Both the plank walkway and the out-house seemed unreachable before disaster would strike. Doubled over, I struggled to reach my boots while keeping my coat from dragging. Suddenly, I felt strong hands clamp around my waist from behind and lift me straight out of my boots. I shouted, "My boots, my boots!"

Then, the hands slowly lowered me enough to put my feet back in the boots and grab the tops. Again, the strong hands lifted me, but this time very slowly to make sure the boots came with me. My rescuer walked me over to the planks and put me down.

Once on solid ground, I had a chance to turn around and see that the hands belonged to a young man. But before I could say anything, he was already walking away. I tried to thank him but I was also very much in a hurry to get to the outhouse. All I saw of him was his back.

I will never know who he was—other than two strong hands that helped me when I needed it. To this day, this memory reminds me of how much small acts of kindness can help others, often more than the person will ever know.

While that stranger helped me to safety when I felt alone and helpless, another man in the camp whom I trusted did me harm. This memory is one I will never forget. I was much too young and innocent to be able to see through his overt kind words and gestures. While one man helped me, the other man helped himself.

If I had wanted to borrow a father, I would have chosen Mr. M. He was a happy man and he called me "cute little Mako." I envied his daughter Susan because her dad looked like the ideal father. At seven, Susan was a little older than me and she also had three older brothers. I was keenly aware that I had neither a father nor a brother with me at the camp. I often thought, *Susan is a lucky girl!*

I saw Mr. M frequently. He came to the girls' dance practice sessions often. His daughter was a pretty good dancer and I worked hard to try to do better than her. Mr. M made nice comments to the dancers when they finished the day's lessons. He was always upbeat, friendly, and complimentary. I would think, *Some people like Susan have all the luck!*

One day after my dance class, I was walking back to our barrack alone. Mr. M took my arm and pulled me aside. I was happy to see his friendly face. He whispered and asked me to meet him by the kitchen door of the mess hall after I finished my dinner. "This is important," he said, "but come alone and don't tell anyone about our meeting."

This was an unusual request and I was flattered that he took such an interest in me. Mr. M's request sounded mysterious and fun, and I was very curious what this meeting might be about. My child imagination grew wild throughout the afternoon. Maybe I would meet the Queen of Hearts or maybe meet a *hakujin* (white) couple. Perhaps this nice couple would want to adopt me and take me away from the camp! A part of me knew that was not realistic, but then again, maybe that *could* happen.

All afternoon I enjoyed imagining what I would do if I were put into such a fortunate situation. I wouldn't want to hurt Mama, but it might be exciting to escape this camp and become a hero helping others escape, too.

That night after dinner, Mr. M waited for me at the mess hall kitchen door, just like he said he would. I can't remember where he led me or how he got me sitting across his lap. I do remember feeling snug and secure with his strong arms across my shoulders. The stubble on his chin rubbed on my forehead and chafed my skin, but I didn't really mind.

In a soothing voice, he spoke of the golden moon, a soft welcoming breeze, and what a lovely child I was. Then, he suddenly kissed my lips and his tongue was in my mouth. I was shocked. I thought, *Is he crazy? He will get my germs and I will get his germs! Yucky!*

I couldn't figure out why he kept sticking his tongue in my mouth—in and out, in and out. *When will he quit?*

What else he did, I'm not sure. Years later, when I understood what was going on, I had played this scene over and over, trying to remember. I might have blanked out on some things that Mr. M did to me because I didn't want to acknowledge them. I did have lots of trouble understanding what he was doing and what it meant.

When Mr. M finally seemed to have finished, he sat back and asked me a strange question: "Did you enjoy the kiss?"

By the way he looked at me, I knew it was an important question. I wanted to answer it correctly because I was told to always be polite to adults. I couldn't think of what to say, so I just said, "Yes."

I thought for sure he would know I was lying, but after a moment, he smiled and said, "That's good." Then he made me promise, "You can't tell anyone about our kiss because they won't understand."

That evening, I tried to figure out Mr. M's puzzling behavior. I did not "understand" our kiss. I did decide he would not kiss his own daughter the same way. I knew I liked his arms around me, I enjoyed sitting on his lap, and I liked his secret attention, but something was unsettling and confusing. I wanted him as a father because he was an adult man who treated me as "special" and I basked in his attention. No adult had ever asked me to promise to keep a secret and even *that* felt special. Yet, feelings of embarrassment and guilt also clouded this strange encounter.

I did not tell Mama about the incident. Actually, I didn't tell anyone because Mr. M said it was our secret. Somehow, I knew this was wrong, and I was quite sure Mama would not approve of the incident. She might have even made a fuss and confronted him. After that incident, Mr. M often winked at me in public when no one was looking or made some other secret recognition of me.

At the time, I did not think Mr. M's behavior was sexual abuse. I simply had no idea of what sex or abuse was; I had led a protected and innocent life up to that point. I just saw it as strange behavior. In hindsight, I was very fortunate that we left Minidoka for Crystal City before Mr. M made another move toward me.

For many years, I did not tell anyone what Mr. M did to me when I was five years old. In a way, I felt it was my duty to keep his secret for him. Somehow, I thought it was my obligation to protect Mr. M from being "misunderstood." Then one day, more than 50 years after the incident, I asked Kazu, "Do you remember Mr. M in Minidoka?"

She promptly responded, "Oh yeah, he was a pedophile."

If I wasn't standing right next to a chair, I would have slid right down to the floor when I heard those words. I grabbed the chair and sat down, asking my sister, "Why do you call that man a pedophile?"

Kazu said, "It just popped out of my mouth."

We just looked at one another for a long pause, then Kazu said, "My friends used to call him Mr. Ickey."

Kazu explained that she didn't know the word "pedophile" in those days, but today that word fits. "He touched the girls and hung on a little longer than he should have," Kazu explained. "He was always staring at the girls with a funny look. One time, he followed one of the girls."

Then Kazu added, "You always wanted someone with you if he was around."

I was astounded. "Wow! Why didn't you tell me?"

Then I thought to myself, *Why didn't I recognize he did indeed molest me?*

At five, I had no idea what any of this meant. It took me over a half a century to realize what had happened. I now know that Mr. M never should have touched me and kissed me the way he did. He was molesting me, not being kind to me. What he did was wrong. To this day, I have a nagging need to tell him that, but he is gone. Dead. Only the nagging need remains.

My first attempt to share my secret was to write the story on paper. I did struggle trying to decide if I should delete the story from the book. I asked myself, *How does Mr. M's behavior relate to the incarceration story?*

For a long time I mulled this over, realizing that I was an older adult by the time I understood the incident as sexual abuse. Not the worst example of sexual abuse, but nonetheless, it was sexual abuse. In the end, I decided, "Hell yes, I'll include this story in my manuscript."

Then I asked myself, *Was it wrong? Hell, yes. Was the incarceration of* Nikkei *into concentration camps wrong? Hell, yes!*

I needed to speak the truth about all the wrongs I experienced in these camps.

I decided this secret had to be told. The secret must end. This, too, was part of the incarceration story. I had been afraid to break a promise I made to Mr. M, but now I knew some promises needed to be broken. I am still haunted with the question, *Why did it take me so long to come to this conclusion?*

During my tenure as an elementary school principal, on occasion I was called upon to be a witness at a meeting between a student and a social worker, reporting cases of sexual abuse. Fortunately, the social workers were top notch in handling difficult situations. In turn, I did my best to be professional, interested, compassionate, and nonjudgmental. After each of these sessions, I must admit it took me a long time to recover from the turmoil churning in my stomach. My instinctive response is that anyone who exploits vulnerable children cannot be redeemed or forgiven. I am against capital punishment, but whenever I had to sit through hearings on sexual abuse, I secretly wanted to yell, "Hang him!"

I now understand that my churning stomach was connected to my own painful past. I do consider abuse of the vulnerable, and the betrayal of trust, as two of the most heartbreaking actions against humanity. Now, I understand and can admit how vulnerable and confused I was in that prison camp so many years ago—and how much I trusted that adults would be kind to me. I also understand that this kind of violation is never forgotten.

CHAPTER 14

SCARCITY & A COOKIE

*M*ama was in the hospital, waiting to bring me into the world, when she ate an entire box of chocolates all by herself. Her "sweet tooth days" began with this pregnancy and ended when she came home cradling me in her arms. Her sudden craving for candy and chocolate never reappeared, but she did manage to leave a lasting legacy for me—a lifelong fondness for sweets. Okay, it's more than that, I am an addicted chocoholic!

In fact, one of my earliest memories is of *Obaachan* (Grandma) with a big smile on her face, secretly giving me lemon drops when Mama wasn't around. I enjoyed the secret kept from Mama as much as the sweet lemon drops, which seemed to be intertwined with Obaachan's love for me. *Obaachan* died before our family was incarcerated, so I was deprived of her love—and her candy supply.

In spite of my history of being a finicky eater, I don't recall being turned off by any specific food served in the camp mess halls. To the contrary, I, along with most of the children, anticipated with great joy the occasional distribution of chocolate-cov-

ered graham cookies. The wonderful chocolate cookies really satisfied my craving for sweets. I did feel a tinge of disloyalty for enjoying the cookies even more than *Obaachan's* lemon drops. But I thought that chocolate-covered graham cookies were the most delicious treat ever created, and I was sure I would never find anything more delectable.

Once, in order to savor this treasure, I carefully wrapped my cookie in a paper napkin from the mess hall and put it away in my pocket to save for the perfect time when I could relish every bite. I'm sure there must have been a big smile on my face when I finally unwrapped the cookie and got ready to sink my teeth into the chewy sweetness.

At that moment, out of nowhere, Nobu swooped down, grabbed the cookie, took a bite, put it back in my hand, and giggled as she ran off. At first I was in shock, speechless, but then I let out a blood-curdling scream that even I didn't recognize. It came from deep within. My sister quickly returned, apologized profusely, hugged me, and even promised to give me her next cookie allotment, but I was inconsolable with rage. I wanted to throw the remaining part of the cookie at her. Only greed kept me from reacting so wastefully.

After my sister's friend found another cookie for me to eat, I finally calmed down. But even with this peace offering, I swore never to trust my sister *ever* again as long as I lived. That's how strongly I felt about the whole incident. At a time when so many people around me felt outrage at the injustice of losing their freedom, their privacy, their property, their dreams, and their loved ones, my outrage was over the loss of one bite of my precious, chocolate-covered graham cookie. At that time in my life, that was one of my greatest treasures.

Years later, while giving a talk to a large audience of high school students, a woman asked me what was the worst thing that happened to me in the concentration camps. The story of my chocolate-covered graham cookie immediately came to mind. A part of me wanted to share a more dramatic experience and a more traumatic loss, but honestly, as a young child enduring the incarceration, this cookie incident loomed large. Perhaps it also reflected a general sense of scarcity and a lack of sweetness in being trapped in the camps.

As an adult, I look at this story and think it's petty and downright silly in contrast to other camp tragedies I learned about in later years. I have read many interviews, testimonials, articles, and reports. I have listened to firsthand accounts that convey so many people's heart-wrenching stories of suffering. There are many stories paid for in blood, sweat, tears, anger, frustration, despair, humiliation, and more. Too many stories are slated to die along with their owners without ever being given a hearing.

So, I pointed out to that high school audience that I was allowed to wallow in my little misery over my cookie only because the adults, facing huge worries and uncertainties, still strived to provide the children in camp a sense of normalcy. Many times over the years I have wondered, *What must the adults have been feeling deep inside? What depth of suffering did they keep from us children?*

Only now do I appreciate the protection that was provided me during those years. Growing up in a concentration camp was made to be as close to "normal" as the adults could manage.

Many children were not as protected as I was from their parents' anger and despair. One day, I walked beyond my block toward my friend's block. Tomoko was more of a listener and I was more of a talker, so we seemed to fit well. After playing for a bit, we walked toward Tomoko's barracks. Before we got to the door to her section of the barracks, her younger brother charged out of the door and ran to Tomoko telling her something I couldn't hear. Right after this whispered message, a man appeared at the door and shouted to Tomoko and her brother to come in. He glared at me but said nothing. Tomoko quietly said, "Sorry," and walked in the door.

I slowly walked back to our quarters in our barrack and kept going over the event I had witnessed. The man, who I assumed was Tomoko's father, was downright scary. What Tomoko and her brother were going through at that moment was a complete mystery to me, but one glance at this angry man and I was definitely scared. I even thought murder was a possibility because he seemed so angry.

Many times I asked myself, *Why do other children have fathers and not me? What will happen to us if we don't have a mother or a father?*

I knew I wanted a father desperately, but I realized that I did not want Tomoko's father. I wanted a nice father. Later, I talked to Tomoko and asked her, "Does he get angry often?"

Tomoko brushed off the question, only saying her father sometimes had a temper. "But he usually gets over it," Tomoko reassured me.

I did not believe her but I didn't ask any more questions. My feeling was he probably hit her, too. After that, I was clear: *Yes, sometimes having a father can be worse than not having a father.*

I can't specify why I felt the dark, heavy, secret anger that I was immersed in during my time at

Minidoka. I was young, but I noticed unhappy adults everywhere in the camps, and I wondered, *Why are the adults so angry and mean to each other?*

Even Mama only laughed rarely now. So many seemed to be sad or arguing constantly. I survived all of this by making up stories of loneliness and wishing for good things to happen. I liked my fantasy world and my grand imagination. My imaginary world gave me great comfort.

CHAPTER 15

OHHH SANTA!

The first Christmas I can remember as a child was in the Minidoka camp. I was coming home from my morning kindergarten class when one of the older girls asked, "Do you believe in Santa?"

I didn't answer, but I thought, *That's a strange question. Of course I believe in Santa.*

Later, I mentioned Santa in a conversation with Mama. Her face turned serious as she sat me down and told me, "I expect you to act like a big girl now. There will be no Santa for you this year. Santas are really fathers trying to make their children happy."

Then she proceeded to tell me that because this was not a happy year for us, I would have to give up on the idea of Santa because Papa could not be with us. I can't remember what else she said. I did as I was told and acted like a "big girl" and did not raise a fuss—at least overtly.

Inside, I was regretting that I had brought up the name of Santa. I was probably lamenting Mama was my mother, too. Later in the day when Nobu came home from school, she happened to say something

about Santa. She was shocked to learn that Mama had revealed his true identity to me. Nobu actually raised her voice to Mama saying, "We could have done something. It's not right to tell Mako there is no Santa!"

I was stunned that Nobu would challenge Mama so openly. But at the same time, I was thrilled. It was easier to bear not getting a present from Santa because my sister was on my side.

Strangely, Mama didn't say a word. She might have looked sad, but I was absorbed in my own sorrows, so I didn't notice. For a long time after that, every time I had a disagreement with Mama, I secretly mumbled *Santa* and put on the most disagreeable face I could muster.

Some 25 years later around Christmas time, I was so relieved when a much-needed student loan check arrived. It was so nice to know I wouldn't have to disappoint my own son with a less costly Santa gift than the one he asked Santa to grant him. With my husband still a student on the G.I. Bill and me pregnant with my second child, money was tight, and I would soon have to give up my job to deliver the baby and care for our new child. I worried, *How am I was going to buy the special Santa present for my five-year-old son Daren?* The student loan was heaven sent.

It was not until the moment Daren joyfully opened his Christmas gift from Santa, beaming as he pranced around the room, that it dawned on me how Mama must have felt when I was five. Did she feel she failed me by not being able to provide Santa who had been whisked out of my life so unreasonably? Was she full of sorrow in her inability to carry the tradition of Santa Claus for me? Did my unhappiness serve to make her feel guilty and inadequate?

For so many years, I held Mama responsible for the sad message about no Santa that she thought she needed to tell me. For the first time since the camp days, I experienced that Santa episode in camp through Mama's eyes. The big smile on my son's face opened a new feeling of empathy for Mama's sorrow as a mother rather than just the disappointment I felt as a child. In that moment of insight, understanding Mama's viewpoint,

I whispered, *"Gomenasai ne.* (I'm really sorry Mom!) I know you forgive me, but let me say I'm sorry anyway."

In 2007, I went on the Minidoka Pilgrimage to see the concentration camp that has since been declared a National Monument. The Minidoka Pilgrimage takes place yearly during the summer months. The elderly attend the event to reminisce, share experiences, and look over the landscape, while a good number of young people want to learn and to connect with the history of the area. The Minidoka Pilgrimage committee works hard to provide a wide range of activities to meet the expectations of those attending. I unintentionally joined the pilgrimage committee at first, but ended up participating for a number of years because I was impressed with the committee's effective work. I could see how much pilgrims benefited from this trip into Japanese American history.

While on one of these pilgrimages, I had the opportunity to talk to Mrs. Shigeko Uno who had been active in the Japanese American community ever since she was a young woman held at Minidoka during the war. I had long admired her active dedication to serving the community and changing the world around her for the better. She was the first woman president of the Seattle Chapter of Japanese American Citizens League (JACL). Shigeko was essentially a "no nonsense doer" with a big heart. She never learned to drive a car, but that didn't stop her from attending meetings and events regarding social justice and civil rights issues. Frankly, I admit I was initially intimidated by her spirited activism, outspokenness, and well-recognized track record. Definitely, I was in awe of her—so much so that I did not have the courage to get too close to her.

After hearing my "Ohhh Santa" story at the pilgrimage, Shigeko approached me and asked if I remembered getting a Santa gift after all. She seemed slightly let down when I told her, "No, I didn't get a Santa gift that year."

She then proceeded to tell me *her* story from the Minidoka days. Her story was a greater gift than any I could have received from Santa.

About the time I was moaning about my loss of a Santa present, Shigeko was a young mother in the camp busy washing diapers, plus other laundry, by hand. Like many other young parents, she constantly worked at keeping her family's small living space clean, wiping down the continual layers of dust in the barracks. She also took turns with her sister to keep the nighttime cries of her baby curtailed so as to not disturb other families in the barrack.

I have heard many stories of imprisoned people becoming depressed, bored, and frustrated. In contrast, Shigeko told me she was much too busy trying to keep up with the daily demands in front of her, as well as thinking about the larger community at Minidoka, especially the children. The idea of a child having to face a Christmas without a Santa gift was more than Shigeko could bear. So, she stretched her energy to join a committee determined to make sure every child in Minidoka received a Christmas present from Santa. The committee wrote to every organization they could think of both in the Minidoka area, outside the camp, as well as in Washington State, soliciting money and suitable gifts for the children. The committee's hard work paid off and they collected enough money and goods to meet their goal.

The next challenge was the distribution of the gifts to the right child. They found a good Santa and matched a gift to the intended child, which was quite a task. As Shigeko told me her story, I marveled at the committee's persistence to achieve their goal at a time when many other challenges were facing the inmates.

It is a mystery why I didn't get my gift from Santa. The news clipping I saw of Santa passing out gifts to children in Minidoka was dated 1944. By then, our family was probably being transferred to the Crystal City camp in Texas. If that was the date that they were able to launch their project, then it is understandable why I missed out on getting a Santa gift that year. I felt somewhat bad for giving Shigeko the disappointing news that I have no memory of benefiting from the Santa project. Still, I was grateful to Shigeko and her Santa Committee for all the children they delighted at Christmas in Minidoka.

There was one more amazing chapter in Shigeko's story that happened decades later. In the 1990s, Shigeko attended a national gathering of Japanese Americans. Out of nowhere, an elderly man, wobbling and walking painfully with a cane, approached her. He verified her name and asked if she was the same Shigeko Uno who served on the committee to get Santa gifts for children in the Minidoka camp. When she said, "Yes," he broke into a big smile and his eyes filled with tears. He asked if he could give Shigeko a hug. The grateful man explained that he had been looking forward to hugging her for many decades. The

Santa gift he got in camp was the very first Christmas gift he had ever received as a young boy. As tears streamed down his face, he told Shigeko he had never in his long life treasured a gift more than that present from Santa while at Minidoka.

Shigeko passed away not long after telling me her story at that pilgrimage in 2007. She was 96 years old. At her memorial service, Shigeko was recognized for a long list of contributions and accomplishments, but I am most pleased that she had gotten that hug from this man while she was still alive and well. And I'm glad he got the opportunity to hug Shigeko and thank her.

And I am ever grateful for the gift of Shigeko's Santa story.

CHAPTER 16

A Call to Arms

While at Minidoka, I knew nothing of the turmoil going on for the adults in the concentration camps and the overall treatment of Japanese Americans in the United States. Years later, I would understand the deep divisions in the country and how Americans of Japanese descent were singled out and discriminated against, even when they wanted to fight for the United States.

The American response to the attack on Pearl Harbor was immediate, widespread, and intensely patriotic, particularly in Hawaii. Droves of young people found their way to the recruiting centers to volunteer for military duty and to serve their country. Not surprisingly, many eager recruits were Americans of Japanese descent. When they tried to sign up to fight for the United States, recruitment officers rejected them solely based on their ethnicity. Young, able-bodied Japanese men were reclassified from I-A to IV-C or "enemy alien," which meant they were unfit for military duty.

When I was researching this time period many years later, I saw an interview with one Japanese American man whom recruitment officers rejected because of his ethnicity. A reporter asked him, "What did you think? How did you feel?"

He confessed he was totally confused and didn't know *what* to think. He said, "I only remember leaving the building and suddenly feeling my knees get weak. I simply sat down on the curb and cried like a baby."

Even the *Nikkei* soldiers who were already actively serving in the U.S. military received letters from the U.S. government terminating their service. They were terminated because they were of Japanese descent and their loyalty to the United States was questioned. At the start of World War II, race and ancestry *did* indeed play a central role, perhaps the sole role, in determining who qualified as a viable American soldier.

When President Franklin D. Roosevelt authorized Executive Order 9066, U.S. Army Lieutenant General John L. DeWitt was given the power to expel some 120,000 thousand *Nikkei* living in the Western United States. DeWitt believed that Japanese and Japanese Americans living in parts of California, Oregon, Washington and Arizona could be conspiring with Japan in its war efforts. He ordered the removal of all *Nikkei* from the coastal areas, even though more than 60 percent were U.S. citizens. Lieutenant General DeWitt testified before the House Naval Affairs Subcommittee and rationalized this gross racial profiling and unconstitutional decision by saying, "A Jap's a Jap. There is no way to determine their loyalty. This coast is too vulnerable. No Jap should come back to this coast except on a permit from my office."

General DeWitt ignored the many highly placed governmental sources that concluded the Japanese living on the West Coast were extremely loyal and an extremely low threat. Those sources included J. Edgar Hoover of the FBI, the Naval Intelligence, and Curtis Munson's covert assessment of loyalty with the Japanese American community. Their conclusions were detailed in "The Report on Japanese on the West Coast of the United States." They all corroborated and concluded the Japanese Americans were extremely loyal, despite Japan's attack on Pearl Harbor.

The U.S. declared war on Japan on December 8, 1941, the day after Japan had bombed Pearl Harbor and declared war on the United States. A couple months later with the authority of Executive Order 9066, the U.S. military began to exclude *Nikkei* soldiers from fighting. Immediately, various individuals and groups sought to find strategies to open up military service for *Nikkei* already in the military and for those who wanted to enlist. Finally in February 1943, President Roosevelt and the U.S. War Department activated a primarily Japanese American unit to fight the battles in Europe.

Nearly a thousand young men of Japanese descent left Minidoka concentration camp to voluntarily serve in the U.S. military. Of the ten major WRA camps, the Japanese American men recruited from Minidoka would eventually suffer the largest number of casualties during World War II.

By the war's end, more than 33,000 Japanese Americans served in the U.S. military during World War II. Initially, many soldiers came from Hawaii where they were already enlisted. They were soon joined by many other young Japanese Americans in the ten U.S. concentration camps—young people who wanted to prove their loyalty to their country, the United States. While they served, their families remained in the confines of the U.S. camps.

The 100th Infantry Battalion represented the first Japanese American soldiers—many of them from Hawaii—to fight in World War II. This brave battalion got the nickname "The Purple Heart Battalion" in recognition of the soldiers' selfless and fierce fighting, dedication, and the high number of battle wounds and deaths they endured. The success of the 100th Infantry Battalion influenced the army to create a *Nisei* combat unit comprised of soldiers of Japanese ancestry. The 442nd Regimental Combat Team included Japanese Americans from all ten of the WRA's concentration camps. About 14,000 men served in the 442nd Regiment whose motto was "Go for Broke." Among them, they earned 9,486 Purple Hearts. By the end of the war, the 100th Infantry Battalion and the 442nd Regimental Combat Team were two of the most decorated groups fighting in World War II. They received about 18,000 individual medals, but it came at a high cost—about 9,500 soldiers killed in battle.

The soldiers of the 100th Battalion/442 Regimental Combat Team, along with the *Nisei* soldiers in the U.S. Military Intelligence Service (MIS), military nurses, and Red Cross workers all believed their exemplary conduct in the military would lay groundwork for future Japanese Americans to enjoy freedom in the United States. About 16,000 young *Nisei* served their country in various capacities during the war, while at the same time many of their family members were held in U.S. concentration camps for Japanese Americans.

In recent times, there is a growing appreciation for the loyalty and sacrifices of Japanese American women who donned uniforms and worked tirelessly to support the men in battle during World War II. Unbelievable gains were made, but at unbelievable human costs— something I tell myself I *must* remember and always be grateful for as a Japanese American woman.

When I was about six or seven, I had vague memories of adults in the camp talking about our "heroes of the war," but I didn't find this very interesting. I did seem to accept that we owed a large debt to these soldiers who fought for us, but quite frankly, what would that mean to a kid? What I visualized when hearing these conversations was far from anything possibly realistic. I visualized the romanticized scenes in the action comic books I had looked at—lots of brave battles, lots of violence, but little pain except for the villains. *Nisei* young men wearing military uniforms, and women in military or Red Cross uniforms visited their families in the camps while on leave. To me, they were courageous, honorable, certainly good looking, and they cared about people who fought hard on behalf of America, including the *Nikkei* people. I felt pride.

Adults also talked about "Gold Star Mothers." I had no idea what the term meant, but I could tell that there was much sadness involved whenever someone mentioned the phrase "Gold Star Mothers." It was somehow connected to the small banners people placed in the windows of a barracks unit. I heard the Japanese version of the "loss" of a son, or that the son was "gone." I concluded that meant a son had "died in battle," as the adults said.

I'm quite sure I had no concept of death during this time but somehow I connected it with disappearing into a puff of smoke. When Grandma had died, the adults told me she was put into a small and pretty vase. *That's silly!* I thought. *Grandma was small but not that small.* The adults seemed to be serious when they explained where *Obaachan* had gone, but it still sounded silly. I knew adults were silly sometimes, so I decided the puff of smoke made better sense than the vase story.

It was much later in my life that I learned a family faced with the death of an immediate member while fighting with enemy forces was given a small banner with one gold star for each member who made the ultimate sacrifice—his life. Each blue star on a little banner signified that a member of the immediate family was actively serving in the armed forces during a war or hostilities.

Uncle Shig was the closest person in our family who was involved with the U.S. military. Mama's younger brother was born in the United States and had never been to Japan. His use of the Japanese language was limited, as was his general knowledge of Japanese culture and history. My sisters and I thought our Uncle Shig was fun, sensitive, handsome, and so charming. He loved country-western music and was pretty good at yodeling, which Mama laughingly described as the sound of a cat being strangled.

In Minidoka, Uncle Shig's wife, Shigeko "Charlotte" Suyetani, had birthed their baby girl, Joyce, in 1943. Shig had already volunteered for the military and he was gone by the time his daughter was born. We were at Minidoka camp with our Auntie Charlotte when her daughter was born. I was fascinated with my brand new Cousin Joyce.

Shig was one of the early volunteers for military duty in the 442nd Regimental Combat Team which had been opened to *Niseis* in January 1943. When Uncle Shig eagerly signed up to fight in the war, Mama worried. She had no objection to Shig enlisting and hoped her little brother would survive his military experience. Reluctantly, she accepted that he was an American and it was his duty to serve now that this option was open to him. While fighting in Europe, he was wounded in battle and became a paraplegic for the rest of his life. As a result, he was unable to father more children, and Joyce was his only child.

I recall Mama being devastated over the news of Uncle Shig's injuries. I felt more sorry for Mama than I did for Uncle Shig. Mama was in front of me everyday with her painful looks, crying, and general sadness for her brother who had been wounded in some faraway place called Italy. Yet, I did feel proud of my Uncle Shig for being so brave and patriotic.

CHAPTER 17

A QUESTION OF LOYALTY

Mama was deeply steeped in her pride of being Japanese even though she had been born in Hawaii. However, she was sent to live in Japan when she was young and raised to be a traditional Japanese woman. She revered the Emperor of Japan but was apolitical, and when Mama came to the United States, she remained uninterested in politics. When Japan and the United States declared war on one another, she was most unhappy. Japan had never lost a war, so Mama assumed that Japan would win the war. Yet the idea of taking up arms against either Japan or America was unthinkable. Mama wished only that the war would end so our family could be reunited with Papa and get back to our previous life.

During the time we lived in the concentration camps, my sisters and I were totally unaware of Mama's right to U.S. citizenship because she was born in Hawaii, a U.S. Territory at the time. Mama may have had dual citizenship, but we don't know for sure. My family can only guess that Mama's parents somehow kept only the Japanese citizenship active and let the American citizenship lapse when Mama went to live in Japan. She felt a deep respect and loyalty to Japan and her ancestors, and yet, she also loved her new country, America. Mama was also of the Shinto faith which gave her much comfort. This devotion to a Japanese way of living would soon tear apart thousands of families imprisoned in the camps—including Mama.

Resentment and anger grew over the injustices and unconstitutional actions against the *Nikkei* in the concentrations camps. Unbearable living conditions, strict rules and daily humiliations led some inmates to protest the unjust treatment. People began demanding their rights as U.S. citizens. The military police at the camps generally dismissed the inmates' concerns and labeled them as "troublemakers" and "disloyal." Some protestors were severely punished; beaten and placed in solitary confinement. At the same time, others in the camps, such as members of the Japanese American Citizens League (JACL), followed the WRA's agenda of assimilation and cooperation as the more reasonable tactic. Many did as they were told. Inmates from opposing sides in the camps clashed frequently and in December 1942 some of the inmates at the Manzanar concentration camp gathered for a protest rally that turned into a riot. The military police fired, without orders, into the fleeing unarmed crowd, killing two people and injuring at least another ten.

In 1943, the unrest in the camps led the WRA and the War Department to devise a plan that they thought would determine which inmates in the camps were loyal to the United States and which were not. Their plan caused even deeper divisions and turmoil among the camp prisoners. The WRA required all *Nikkei* seventeen years or older to fill out and submit a questionnaire later dubbed the "Loyalty Questionnaire." This immediately caused an explosion of confusion among inmates in all of the camps. Many *Nikkei* questioned the purpose of the questionnaire, resulting in the inmates writing a long list of concerns, questions, objections, legal challenges, and more.

The inmates talked about the questionnaire continuously, whether they were in the mess hall, the laundry room, latrines, and certainly in whispered tones in their living quarters. Often, heated arguments erupted and tension within families and among inmates simmered. Even as a six year old, I could sense the mounting tension connected to the questionnaire. At the time, I was completely oblivious to what all the adult talking was about. I didn't understand what was going on, but I could *feel* the anger and confusion.

In our family, since Mama was the only adult with four young daughters, the controversial issue of proving our loyalty was not an option. No one in our family had to grapple with the decision whether or not to join the U.S. military. We also did not want to renounce our American citizenship and volunteer to be deported to Japan. Our young family was focused on surviving life in the camps and being reunited with Papa.

As an adult, I began to understand why the adults in the camps were in so much turmoil over the "Loyalty Questionnaire" and its implications. I also learned that the hard feelings among Japanese Americans formed

then, continued to fester in the community decades after the end of the war. For some, more than 70 years later and it is still a painful topic.

The immediate concerns in the Loyalty Oath were over question 27 and question 28. These two questions originally read:

27. Are you willing to serve in the armed forces of the United States on combat duty, wherever ordered?
28. Will you swear unqualified allegiance to the United States of America and faithfully defend the United States from any or all attack by foreign or domestic forces, and forswear any form of allegiance or obedience to the Japanese emperor, or any other foreign government, power, or organization?

What the WRA considered "simple questions" regarding loyalty, actually turned into numerous questions among most of the *Nikkei* in the camps required to sign this oath. The confusion and uncertainty led to daily debates. Many others asked questions such as:

- What was the purpose of the questionnaire?
- Wouldn't an *Issei* foreswearing allegiance to the Japanese emperor be tantamount to becoming a person with no country?
- Did foreswearing allegiance to the Japanese emperor mean a person is admitting to once having had that allegiance?
- Did answering "yes" and "yes" to questions 27 and 28 mean that they had volunteered for military duty?
- What would be the consequence of a *Nisei* responding "no" and "no" to the two questions?

- What consequence would a "Yes/No" or a "No/Yes" response bring about?
- What would happen if an addendum statement is added saying they would be very willing to sign "yes' and "yes" provided they were treated with equity along with other US citizens?

Isseis successfully petitioned the WRA to have Question 28 revised to read:

28. Will you swear to abide by the laws of the United States and take no action which would in any way interfere with the war effort of the United States?

Subsequently, the respondents who answered questions 27 and 28 with a "no" and a "no" were labeled disloyal. About 20,000 refused to answer the questions, or they qualified their answers, or they answered one or both of the questions with a "no." Anyone with a "no" on either question was also considered "disloyal" to the United States regardless of *why* they chose this response. Inmates from the nine WRA camps who responded "no" to one or both questions were transferred to the Tule Lake camp, which was redesignated the "Tule Lake Segregation Camp." Residents already at Tule Lake who had responded "yes yes" were allowed to transfer to one of the WRA camps. Some chose to stay at Tule Lake rather than transfer to a new WRA camp.

Anyone imprisoned in Tule Lake could be suddenly picked up and forced into the stockade facility, ignoring the right of due process for those who were U.S. citizens. In addition, camp authorities covertly pressured many U.S. citizens at Tule Lake into giving up their American citizenship. I knew very little about the men in the camps who refused to join the military, and what I did hear was painfully inaccurate. I recall associating the "no-no boys" with embarrassment and disgrace. They were spoken about in hushed terms in front of us kids. Many of the *Nikkei* in the camp labeled the "no-no boys" as disloyal, frequently even calling them cowards. I accepted the general sentiment among many in the camps that it was dishonorable and cowardly to refuse to fight during World War II.

A good number of these men were not only vilified by the American government, but many people within the mainstream *Nikkei* population often turned their backs on the "no-no boys" and shunned them. Those who brought their cases before the U.S. courts often found their positions summarily ignored with various penalties assessed. The country's anti-Japanese sentiment was prevalent to the point where even judges publicly used the demeaning term "Japs" when referring to them in court for a hearing.

During those times, I recall often being asked the perennial question adults ask kids: "What do you want to be when you grow up?"

A truthful response would have been, "I don't want to become an adult."

From my perspective, the adult world seemed full of anger and pain. I knew an honest response would not be proper for me to confess, so I made up responses based on my fantasy world. "I want to be a princess," I'd answer, or maybe, "I want my fairy godmother to give me lots of toys." Adults smiled at my responses and patted me on the head. If I had confessed the truth—that I didn't want to "grow up"—the adults would have frowned.

All of these adult, soul-searching struggles, pressured decisions, and agonies floated right over my head. All I remember is the increased tension among the adults. Verbal battles and flareups were common. Angered adults were often oblivious to children within earshot. Hearing Japanese curse words heatedly spoken about became almost routine—words that I only understood as "bad."

I knew the proper word for white people was *hakujin*. Even at six years old, I also knew many of the differences between the *hakujins* ('them') and *nihonjin* (us). We kids were instructed to be wary of' "them." Given our situation, I could understand Mama's cautionary warnings about "them."

More than seven decades after this chapter in American history, I still reflect on all the emotional turmoil within the hearts and minds of the incarcerated people over the issue of military service to our country. I have often wondered what I would have chosen if I had been a young man forced to decide. Would I have shamed my family with my refusal to serve and be labeled a "no-no boy"? Or would I have been a "yes-yes boy" who went to war for my country, even though our country put us in concentration camps solely based on our Japanese ancestry?

By the time I was reading about this infamous Loyalty Questionnaire, I was beyond college age and the war was long over. I do remember feeling a slow burn over the injustice. I noted that many *Nikkei* were in full support of the "yes-yes boys," and the "yes-yes" supporters often harshly judged the "no-no boys." With more information about the Loyalty Oath debacle, I slowly began switching from blind support for those who chose to serve in the military to outrage at the U.S. government for putting my people in this position. Many times I have thought, *How can the government expect people who they claimed couldn't be trusted to walk the streets of Seattle, suddenly be asked to carry rifles and put their own lives in jeopardy and fight for this country? How could the government expect these men to fight for their country while, at the same time, their own families languished in American concentration camps?*

Some of the *Nikkei* in concentration camps who declined to serve in the military had a wide range of reasons for their actions. It has been a great disservice to lump them all together as simply the "no-no boys." In the late 1990s, I participated in a teachers' workshop in Powell, Wyoming, focusing on the imprisonment of Japanese Americans during World War II. One of the groups, the Fair Play Committee, gave a moving presentation on the military service controversy for *Nikkei* incarcerated in the camps. I was fortunate to meet a number of key people who had been resisters and stood firm against serving in the military until their rights were honored. The teachers responded favorably to the workshop and the resisters' issues. This presentation inspired the idea for a conference based solely on the role of the resisters, the ones called the "no-no boys."

In 2002, conference organizers asked me to participate in a conference titled "Protest & Resistance— an American Tradition." Over the years, I've attended and participated in many workshops, conferences, and symposiums on the imprisonment of Japanese Americans during World War II, but this particular conference was a truly impressive and earth-shattering event for me. Through my organizing assignment, I met and worked with people involved in the Loyalty Questionnaire, specifically the ones who answered "no-no."

I was the moderator for two panels on the "no-no boys." It was an honor but also a nerve-racking burden to make sure I did justice to these men who were courageous in their own right. The firsthand stories from the resisters were spellbinding. Each speaker shared his story with genuine openness, clarity, and courage.

A panel for the families of resisters followed, which was equally impressive, but seemed even more touching in that we did not expect such riveting stories. Their presentations were filled with laughter, frustration, and buckets of tears. During both panels, I had all the speakers seated on the stage. I added an extra chair and kept it empty. When all the speakers finished their presentations, I pointed out the empty chair and explained, "Seated in that empty chair are the invisible people who cannot join the others and share their stories because their experiences are beyond the ability to convey what happened.

"Their stories need to be heard, and should be heard, but cannot be heard. These people are sitting at windows of asylums looking out blankly at nothing, or they have already ended their lives, or they are attacking their wives in unexplained anger, or abusing alcohol and drugs. These are the people who have lost their ability to communicate."

There was rapt attention as I spoke about the silenced people and their untold stories. I knew it must be acknowledged that those of us who can share our stories are functional people. And we must remember that there are many stories we will never hear because the silenced people cannot speak their truths. I concluded the second panel discussion noting, "We need to remember the silenced people exist—or existed. We must hold what we know of their stories close to our hearts."

I was apprehensive about what kind of reaction I would get from the audience. I dreaded the possibility that some people may be insulted with this closure. I saw a few tears. It seemed everyone related to the invisible person in the empty chair. Afterward, a number of people told me they knew who was sitting in that empty chair. One man said, "That was my uncle. No one deserves that chair better than him." Another told me, "It was the JACL that was in the chair." One participant tearfully explained, "My brother finally told his story from that chair...." Each person had a story.

Since that conference, I continued to use the "empty chair" idea to acknowledge all those people who have been silenced for a variety of reasons. Many have shared heartrending stories on behalf of those in the empty chair.

Now, I begin to understand the position of the "no-no" men. They are designated as "resisters of conscience" because they stood up for the U.S. Constitution and their rights as American citizens. These people also deserve my admiration and gratitude for their courageous stance. The resisters' actions *protected* our Constitution as much as the men who decided to serve in the U.S. military. I now see *all Niseis* are truly courageous heroes! All of them paved the way—too often with their lives—to make my life easier after the war, and opened many doors of opportunity for Japanese Americans like me. Ultimately, their contributions to further justice benefited all U.S. citizens; when justice prevails, everyone benefits.

Finally, so many years after the Loyalty Oath tore apart families and communities within the camps, I was able to put away the question of "Which group was right?"

Both sides have a perfect right to voice their position on the perplexing issues surrounding the Loyalty Questionnaire and say why each of them made certain choices. Now, I realize that no one should have to make the decisions that Japanese Americans faced when the U.S. government required them to sign the Loyalty Oath.

There is progress in reconciliation, but progress is slow. One man told me he believes the only way there will be closure with this issue is when all the people affected are gone from the earth. I am my father's daughter; I am an optimist. I think education will help all sides reach out and strive to understand these times through more generous hearts and minds. Bridges can be rebuilt within the Japanese American community and within our nation—before we all die.

CHAPTER 18

HEEBIE JEEBIE STORIES

Whenever the adults gathered in a tight circle and talked in subdued tones in the mess hall, we kids guessed they were sharing *hinotama* stories—(*balls of fire coming from a recently departed person*)—or other scary tales. Sometimes, they would stop talking when they noticed us kids within hearing distance. Then again, sometimes they would ignore us and continue taking turns sharing scary stories and commenting on them.

One evening after dinner, several of us kids pretended to be engrossed in a card game of "Concentration" as we moved our game closer toward the circle of adults. We were delighted to get an earful of vivid and creepy stories. The adults' discussions following the stories were often equally as interesting. We younger children huddled close together to protect ourselves from the unknown. I couldn't stop thinking about the scary images from these stories that settled in my mind.

Hinotamas were fireballs that floated through the air, embodying the spirit of a person who had just entered into the next world. Many people who shared these stories claimed to have personally seen a *hinotama*.

Some *hinotama* stories made me laugh, some made me wonder, and some kept me up at night—scared! It was the *hinotama* stories that made me a permanent coward. One night after hearing some scary stories, I cried out in my sleep loud enough to wake up Mama. When I woke up, I was warm with sweat and Mama was hugging and comforting me. Luckily, my sisters didn't wake up. I didn't want them to see me quivering with fear. The best part was that wonderful feeling of being safe in Mama's arms. Maybe Mama was right about one thing though— some things were meant for only adults.

One man told a story claiming he actually saw the *hinotama* coming toward him as he struggled to rush out of its path. He described his panic as if it were happening right then. Just as the *hinotama* reached him, the man ducked, but it brushed his ear as it drifted by. He described the ball of fire as a freezing mass of flashing images. He felt enveloped by the *hinotama* and thought he would disappear and never be heard from again. He told all who were listening, "I felt lucky to have survived."

Hearing this story, a few listeners slowly shook their heads, not entirely believing the story. Others nodded their heads knowingly, recognizing this as the normal behavior of the *hinotama*. One listener commended the storyteller on his survival and then he told his own *hinotama* story. The sharing session continued for a long time. One man spoke about a *hinotama* that flowed into the door of the laundry room at the camp. A number of women claimed they saw that *hinotama* as it made its way through the laundry room and right out the door on the other end. This caused quite a commotion and silenced many skeptics.

My friend Hideo Watanabe told me that he and a group of boys frequently parked themselves outside the camp hospital hoping to see a *hinotama* for themselves. They thought the hospital was the most logical place for a sighting. They devoted long hours waiting for just a glimpse, but they never saw one. I find it interesting that they were convinced of the existence of the *hinotama*, but they just couldn't find the right place at the right time to catch a glimpse.

Before the concentration camps, Papa was the family storyteller. Yet, when it came to stories of spirits and eerie tales from Japan, Mama was the teller of the traditional tales, selecting stories more suitable for children. I learned that in Japan, *tanuki* (badgers) were often equipped with awesome powers. Most of the time the *tanuki* were simply mischievous or playful, and these stories were charming. These badgers had the odd behavior of using their stomachs as drums to communicate with each other over long distances. They could also be mysterious and threatening to people. If the *tanuki* got angry, they could trick a person into dangerously believing there was a bridge across a ravine. Some claimed that *tanuki* hurt and even killed the people they played tricks on.

I was intrigued with all these stories but also a bit leery of the *tanuki*—whatever they were. I was also told I had to be careful of the *kitsune* (fox). Foxes also possessed powers that could fool people. In my active imagination I often wondered, *Was it a fox, or was it a wolf that fooled Little Red Riding Hood?*

I enjoyed fanciful stories, whatever their origin. But for the most part, they were pretty tame compared to the more adult stories circulating around the camp. These stories made my scalp tingle. Even scarier than the stories themselves was the fear the adult storytellers conveyed. Each person appeared to be immersed in the reality of his or her own experience with the scary unknown. As a child, I absolutely believed what the adults were saying.

Besides the *hinotama* stories, the evenings were filled with other stories. One night near midnight, unbeknownst to Mama, my two older sisters slipped out of the barracks to meet up with friends. They were on a mission to verify a rumor that each night at midnight a woman appeared at the corner outside a specific barrack. This woman was reported to sob uncontrollably for a few moments over the loss of her baby and then disappear. I knew about this planned escapade, but I wasn't invited to join my big sisters. Usually, I wasn't a good sport about being left out but this time I was relieved. I didn't want to decline their invitation and look like a chicken. The next morning, my sisters told me the woman did not appear as expected. I wondered if they were telling me the truth or if they were just trying to protect me from having nightmares again. Mama was never the wiser about the naughty outing.

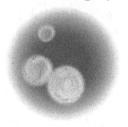

One story got widespread attention—it was about *the photo* in the *Minidoka Interlude 1943 Yearbook*. To this day, many people swear that in one group photo, there is an image of a baby on the chest of a man who had recently lost a child. The people standing with the man that day insisted there was no baby included in the photo. Many of us, adults and children alike, wondered, *How did that image come to be?*

Some people concluded it must have been a photographic trick with lighting. Others shuddered and shook their heads. To this day, many believe the image is a loving message from the deceased child. At the time, the mystery around this photo caused quite a commotion throughout Minidoka. All I know is that it raised goose bumps on me whenever I heard people talk about it.

Today, I find it amazing that Japanese Americans who had been imprisoned at Minidoka more than seven decades ago still discuss the controversy over that particular photo. On the 2007 Pilgrimage to Minidoka, copies of *The Interlude* were sold at the National Monument. Children, and even grandchildren of former Minidoka inmates, were all turning right to the page of the controversial image. They were well informed, prepared with magnifying glasses to scrutinize the evidence—more generations of people to be spooked and chilled by the unexplainable.

During times of prolonged stress, it has been suggested that a close-knit community often times has a corresponding rise in interest of ghostly tales. Perhaps the flight into another world allows people the comfort of a distraction. Could this be the explanation for the wide circulation of *hinotama* and other such stories in the Minidoka camp? There is no doubt that a distraction from the woes of being a prisoner would be a welcomed relief. Maybe focusing on issues beyond this world, rather than face the reality of life in a concentration camp, provided a needed reprieve.

To this day, I am fascinated with younger generations' interest in what they call "heebie jeebie" stories. I am absolutely repulsed by horror films, and I abhor gruesome, violent, and brutal images on television. However, I thoroughly enjoy being eerily disturbed by some mysterious and unexplainable situations. I still love scary stories, and I remain an emotional wimp. Still, I am the frightened child who Mama had to comfort in the middle of the night. But now, I don't mind if my sisters know. They're scared, too—they just hide it better.

This photo of Mama and Papa is the one Mama used
to keep Papa's presence with us.

CHAPTER 19

KEEPING PAPA'S MEMORY ALIVE

During our two-year separation from Papa, my parents were in communication, even if their letters were heavily censored and delayed. Mama worried about her health, afraid if she got sick and died, she would leave their daughters orphans. Mama felt her life energy dwindling, trying to single-handedly care for four young daughters in the concentration camp setting. Maybe it was hard on Mama because she often felt ill, her energy zapped, and she was physically and emotionally drained. She desperately wanted to be reunited with Papa, so she began an urgent plea to reunite her family. Mama persevered with the camp administration to grant her request to reunite with her husband.

Years later, I learned that Mama had signed papers declaring her and her daughters as willing to be part of a prisoner exchange with Japan where we would be reclassified as "Volunteer Civilian Prisoner of War." We assumed this was part of the process of family reunification, and we would be part of an exchange for American soldiers if that opportunity became available.

Initially, Mama was approved to move the family to Tule Lake camp, which had the reputation of being pro-Japanese and the camp that held the *Nikkei* "disloyals." As an adult, I believe Mama was solely interested in the reunification of the family, and which camp we were shipped to did not matter much. Somehow, in the end we were reassigned to a camp near Crystal City, Texas, where we would be reunited with Papa. Finally, Mama's unbelievable persistence in the face of repeated denials got her the approval to meet up with Papa.

After almost two long, hard years in Puyallup and Minidoka, the thought of Crystal City camp in Texas was an exciting change. More than anything else, we would get Papa back in the family. I was so young when Papa was taken away, my memories of the real person were vague, at best. For me, Papa was a photo of a well-groomed man in a tuxedo standing next to my seated mother in what I assumed was their wedding photo. Both my parents looked very distinguished in the photo. Decades later, I learned this photo was taken when Papa was part of a friend's wedding party. Mama kept that special photo on a crate in our living quarters so we could look at it every day. At barely seven years old, that's what I thought of Papa.

Mama's discipline often included her pointing to Papa's photo to emphasize how disappointed he would be to hear of our misbehavior. Mama didn't like us reading comic books, so when Mama scolded us, she'd point to the Papa photo and declare, "Certainly Papa will disapprove of your reading silly comic books." I admit, Papa *did* look rather somber in the photo, but in reality, Papa used to be a fun-loving person not above enjoying practical jokes.

Mama and my sisters talked about Papa constantly, so in my imagination I had a grand image of my papa.

However, I was unable to participate fully in these conversations because my memory of Papa had faded. As the time of our transfer to the Crystal City concentration camp drew near, my family talked about Papa even more often. My sisters were joyful at the thought of being reunited with Papa. Apparently, this was the man who sent letters to Mama that she seemed to treasure. It made no difference that large portions of these letters were blacked out by government censors. Papa also managed to send pine nuts, which were new to us and which I thoroughly enjoyed.

We not only spoke of what Papa wrote but we spent many hours talking about what he probably *really* wanted to write. On two occasions, Papa even sent wooden trunks, each one handmade by a fellow inmate. The first trunk Papa sent had Kazu's name carved on it. When the second trunk arrived, it had Nobu's name on it. I was *sure* the next trunk would have my name but that never happened. I was sad about this and even though I didn't remember Papa, I still wanted him to have a trunk made for me. *Poor me!*

Finally, Mama got permission to leave Minidoka and signed papers to transfer our family to another camp. After almost two years at Minidoka, we left on August 21, 1944 for "Crystal City Alien Enemy Detention Facility," about 110 miles south of San Antonio. My sisters were overjoyed at the thought of going to Texas where we would be with Papa again. I was excited, too, but at the same time, I did harbor some reservations. I thought about something I might need to tell Papa: *Maybe I will remind him that I never got my trunk.*

ILLUSTRATION: MITS KATAYAMA

CHAPTER 20

CRYSTAL CITY CAMP & PAPA

*E*xactly how we got all the way to Crystal City more than 1,500 miles away from Minidoka, I don't remember. All I can recall are long, uncomfortable bus rides and at least one long train ride. However, along the way there were some unforgettable memories. One in particular I would never forget. By seven years old, I was aware of the hatred toward the Japanese. Before that, bigotry had never been obvious or personal for me—but all of that changed at the train station.

A number of armed military guards assigned to escort a group of families in the transfer to Texas, including our family, were initially rude and gruff. They asserted their authority by brandishing rifles and insulting some of the people in our group with their tough tones and orders. The soldiers were constantly counting us to make sure no one had escaped. Mama, along with other members of the group, bristled at the rudeness and humiliation of being pointed at and being ordered to count off verbally, again and again. "That's just the way they would count pigs in Japan," the Japanese women lamented among themselves. The undignified counting off disturbed the older Japanese more than the younger people.

By the time we reached the train station in Portland, Oregon, the guards relaxed their attitudes and the repetitious counting of our group members. They even gave us some time to roam freely around the train station, making sure everyone knew the time and place where we were to regroup. My two older sisters had Mama's permission to climb the huge staircases to the top floor and look down into the main station area. My sisters jumped at the chance to get away from the scrutiny of the guards, and from Mama, and feel a bit of independence.

Mama was probably wise to let my sisters roam a bit, but I was not happy about being excluded from the adventure. I was even more disappointed when they came back and gloated about the view they had from above. "You looked like ants," my sisters observed. I vowed that one day I, too, would be able to look down from a place so high that people would look like ants.

Mama delegated responsibility for the care of three-year-old Midori to my older sisters, and she invited me to go to the ladies' room with her. This was not much consolation, but I was happy to be going *somewhere*. As I walked away with Mama, out of nowhere, a woman jumped out at us calling Mama a "dirty Jap" and then she spit on her. She glared at Mama with eyes full of anger and hate. Then those eyes shifted to me. I clearly saw what I call today the "Naked Eye Look." When her eyes met mine, I thought I saw a small flicker of embarrassment because a child observed her terrible and disrespectful behavior. I had never witnessed anything like this, but I knew the word "Jap" was a forbidden term. In

that split second, Mama kept her composure, took my hand, and we quietly walked to the restroom.

I thought Mama didn't realize the angry woman spit on her until I saw Mama quietly take a paper towel and clean the spot on her coat where the spit had landed. After Mama had thoroughly cleaned off the spit, she threw away the towel, then stooped down and looked intensely into my eyes for a few long seconds. Not a word was spoken. That look meant that I was never to talk about what I had just witnessed—like it never happened.

Before long, the joy of seeing Papa again filled my head, but I never forgot what happened that day. It was not until after Mama died many years later that I even recalled this incident sufficiently to share with my sisters. This humiliation had stayed buried for at least half a century until after 1992 when Mama died at the age of 90. It is strange that this incident never came up for all those years, and yet, when I did speak about it, I recalled it as a detailed memory. At first, it seemed like a dream as I was sharing it with my sisters, and then slowly, I just knew it was real.

The last leg of our trip to the Crystal City Camp was in a hot, stuffy bus on a bumpy road. The dust was thick and stuck to our damp, sweaty skin. Swarming insects added to our discomfort. To make matters worse, we children had to sit on two-by-four boards placed across the aisles on the crowded bus. We tried to balance ourselves while bouncing on a stiff board with rough edges that threatened to give us slivers. The ride seemed much longer than it probably was. I envied Midori who got to sit on Mama's lap. Mama tried to distract us by pointing out the window at different things, but there was very little of interest out there. The tumbleweeds that were fun to see at first, soon became plain boring.

When we finally passed through the gate and barbed-wire fences at the camp, a group of waiting men started to crowd around the bus. Mama changed her distraction game to "Who will be the first to spot Papa"?

I expected Papa to look like he did in the photo and searched for a well-dressed, distinguished man among the group of ragged, dusty-looking people. Hearing my sisters shout, "There he is! There he is!" surprised me because no one in this crowd looked at all well-dressed.

Soon, a man who looked nothing like the man in our cherished photo was holding Nobu's hand through the bus window and calling her Kazu. Nobu laughingly corrected him, pointing to our older sister Kazu, now two years older than when Papa last saw her. Nobu and Kazu were crying and screaming joyously and Papa had tears, too. I figured out that this man, indeed, *must* be Papa, but I was sorely disappointed even to the point of feeling betrayed. I thought to myself, *How could the family be so joyful in being reunited with this raggedy man? Mama was right—Papa had changed, but the change was decidedly for the worse. What a huge letdown!*

Midori, who was now nearly four years old, had a little speech prepared for Papa. She had practiced it hundreds of times on our journey to Texas.

Otoosan, watakushi wa Midori desu. Ookiku natta desho? (Father, I am Midori. Didn't I get big?)

She recited it perfectly and didn't stumble even once. However, Midori wanted no part of this new addition to our family. She clung to Mama and cried every time Papa approached her. I wished I could have run away from Papa like Midori did. I had longed for a father for the whole two years we were at Minidoka, but this man was not the father I had dreamed about. I thought, *Maybe it would be better to have no father at all.*

I didn't understand Kazu's and Nobu's joy to have Papa back in the family. Mama, too, was probably very happy, though I didn't notice her joy at the time. Despite the festive mood around me, I felt isolated and ignored.

When we got to our new living quarters, my sisters were euphoric when they found comic books among Papa's belongings in his suitcase. He was definitely the "old Papa" to them. Papa was a kind and generous man— he had a "soft spot'" for old people and for children.

In contrast with the other camps, Crystal City had many more amenities. The U.S. government thought that if the prisoner exchange between the United States and Japan came to pass, the Crystal City camp inmates would report to the Japanese government that they were treated well during their stay. The U.S. government's thinking was that hopefully, the Japanese government would respond in-kind to their American prisoners.

The Immigration and Naturalization Service (INS) was the official administrator of the Crystal City camp, whereas the WRA had authority over the other concentration camps where we had been incarcerated. Crystal City included both U.S. citizens and noncitizens from several nationalities and from different countries. When the camp had been constructed in November 1942, a ten-foot-high fence surrounded it with floodlights along the perimeter. Armed guards patrolled the grounds, controlling prisoners who were primarily of Japanese ancestry, but included prisoners of German and Italian ancestry. At the height of the camp's population in December 1945, there were 2,313 prisoners of Japanese ancestry, 979 prisoners of German ancestry and 8 prisoners of Italian ancestry.

Crystal City remained a concentration camp but adjustments had been made to improve the comfort of the inmates. We were housed in a duplex unit and not the long barracks we had lived in for about two years. There was a toilet between the two family units and there was a door with a hook-and-eye lock on both sides. When using the toilet, I could lock both doors while still sitting and have some privacy. After the undignified bathroom situations in other camps, it was a stupendous luxury to have one toilet for our family of six and a family of five in the adjoining unit. Eleven people shared one toilet, but we felt as if we had one toilet *all to* ourselves. My family was overjoyed. It would have been great to have a sink and a shower too, but I knew that was asking for the moon.

Another luxury at Crystal City was running water in the housing units. We also had a kerosene stove to cook our own meals in our living space. That meant no more chaotic mess hall meals and long lines. Families used cash vouchers to buy their own food. For my family, this would be a substantial improvement and much appreciated after the miseries of Minidoka.

The administrators at the camp referred to Mama and Papa as "Mr. Takahashi" and "Mrs. Takahashi," rather than by a family number or by their given first name, both of which were considered quite rude in Japanese culture. Mama and Papa took great pleasure in this simple act of respect.

Our new living situation was much improved even though we were still in a prison, held against our will. We were reunited with Papa, finally, and Mama and my older sisters were happy at last. For me, the unrestrained love and trust I had shown when I visited Papa at the INS jail two years earlier had disappeared. I was now seven and filled with disdain and suspicion. I studiously avoided Papa who was now virtually a stranger to me. No, he was more than a stranger—he was an intruder to our family and a threat to my comfort.

Later, Papa told us the story of what happened to him after the FBI took him away. He went from the INS facility in Seattle to Missoula, Montana, where U.S. government officials interrogated him. Papa told us that each of the prisoners got one egg for breakfast which they all savored. Each of them ate his egg slowly, delighted with each bite. Papa said he never knew an egg could taste so good.

After an interrogation session that the military called "a hearing," some men were released and free to return home, or they were sent to the concentration camp where their family was being held. Papa was not among those who were released. He was never made aware of any crime for which he might be culpable. He also was never told why he was denied release. Instead, Papa was transferred from Missoula to Livingston, Louisiana, then on to a prisoner of war camp in Santa Fe, New Mexico.

Each stop was another camp, much like the last. Papa was never told why he was being transferred from camp to camp. He did note that at one of the camps a guard spoke to the prisoners in Japanese. He said, *"Minasan, Yoo koso oide kudasaimashita!"*

The rough translation was, "Gentlemen, we are most honored to have your presence here today." The guard then gave a great bow, a gesture of respect that dumbfounded the prisoners. The overly proper and lavish welcome left the *Nikkei* prisoners speechless. For many months following that unusual and unexpected greeting, the prisoners had various conjectures as to the guard's intent with this flamboyant welcome under the circumstances.

We had followed Papa's moves from one camp to the next by the mail he sent us, each letter a joyful occasion. Papa talked of long days of boredom in the various camps and his longing to be with his family. His thoughts were fully on the reunion with his family, and his sole fear was the possible cancellation of being reunited with us. That would be the cruelest fate of all—a fate he feared he couldn't bear. In the interim, each move to another camp seemed to put Papa further and further away from us.

Mama kept telling us that Papa was not the same man who had been taken from us. His experiences over the previous two years were bound to have made him a much more serious and wise person. Now that we were reunited with Papa, he felt like a stranger to me and I was not comfortable being around him.

Years later, I find it difficult to reconcile how my feelings toward Papa changed so drastically in the almost two years of his absence from my life. When people talk about the losses suffered during those years, the loss caused by the suspension of love and trust is usually overlooked. I believe the most hurtful losses were those that cannot be quantified. How does one mark the loss of ability to plan for the future? Or to wait, not knowing what it is that you are waiting for? Or to forget how to walk tall, or to feel one's self-respect and dignity? Or to see your father and to feel comfortable with him?

When Papa was in his eighties, he talked with me about how he had tried to hide his hurt feelings when his younger daughters were afraid and disdainful of him after we had been reunited in Crystal City. At the time, I was completely oblivious of his feelings toward us. He tried a number of tactics to win over Midori and me. I thought I had masked my distaste of him quite well, but he seemed to have known all along that he needed to work to gain my trust. Fortunately, as it turned out, I was amazingly easy to win over.

Papa was a reader. Every evening before dinner, he would read me Japanese fairy tales and later, Japanese science fiction adventures. Where he got these books is a mystery to me. I loved these stories and it didn't take long for me to comfortably snuggle into his lap, and enjoy his voice and the lingering tobacco scent on his fingers. That is how I first became reacquainted with my father and let down the barrier that I had set up between us. This led to a complete change of heart. In a short time, I became his shadow, following him every-where possible, in complete admiration. He became a hero to me—my best friend and confidant.

A family story goes that when we celebrated Papa's birthday in Crystal City camp, my sisters found me crying. Apparently, I learned that this was Papa's 50th birthday. I reasoned that 50 was half of 100 and people die at 100. My tears were for losing Papa. Fortunately, my family's cavalier attitude about Papa's age reassured me that when Papa turned 100, it would be many, many years away.

My sister Midori stubbornly refused Papa's attention for a long time, but then she, too, finally capitulated to his charm and love even though she remained "Mama's baby." We eventually learned Papa was indeed a lot more than just a distinguished looking man in a photo. Mama became markedly happier and healthier when we were reunited with Papa. This was the family Mama longed for, and at last, we were together again.

CHAPTER 21

DAILY LIFE IN A NEW CAMP

The Crystal City camp was named after the nearby town, Crystal City, Texas, a small farming and ranching community where a statue of the cartoon character Popeye stood prominently in the town square. Popeye was the symbol for a town that boasted to be the "Spinach Capital of the World" and hosted an annual Spinach Festival until the war broke out.

The camp was originally a migratory farm workers' camp that the U.S. government purchased to hold civilian prisoners. The area was far away from any important war production sites and it had a good water supply. There was even a 250-foot-wide swimming pool built by prisoners at the camp.

The endless rows of familiar barracks of Minidoka or Puyallup were nowhere to be seen at Crystal City. In many ways, the Crystal City concentration camp resembled a bustling small town with many amenities. The INS designed Crystal City camp much like a small community with numerous buildings for food stores, auditoriums, warehouses, administration offices, and a 70-bed hospital. There were places of worship, a post office, bakery, barbershop, beauty shop, a school system, a Japanese Sumo wrestling ring, and a German beer garden. Internees printed four camp newspapers in four languages: English, Japanese, Spanish, and German.

The other camps did not have many of the amenities we had at Crystal City, which felt like luxuries at the time. It was rumored among the adults at Crystal City that they were being treated so well because many of our families had already agreed to a prisoner exchange for American soldiers. Fortunately for my family, that did not happen.

Crystal City camp had a large contingency of Buddhist ministers available for the prisoners, but they were prohibited from using Japanese at public services. Mama was of the Shinto faith, which the camp administration discouraged but that didn't stop Mama. Her faith brought her great comfort, and I remember her practicing her daily Shinto rituals, ignoring any public prohibition. Papa was respectful of all faiths but didn't adhere to any particular religion.

Both Mama and Papa were fairly open about our religious beliefs. They were supportive of my attending Buddhist services, so I rarely missed Sunday school. The religious lessons were often taught through stories. A series of colorful drawings were set inside a handmade "stage" just large enough to contain the illustrations. The teacher would tell lively and engaging stories filled with moral lessons. As the story progressed, the pictures would change as the storyteller removed one more illustrated page. This type of theatrics was called *kamishibai*, or paper drama. I loved these stories and loathed to miss a Sunday session.

Japanese school was available and most students seemed eager to attend after completing their American school on weekdays. Japanese school held sessions on Saturday, too. If we chose to attend Sunday school, it was possible to attend school everyday of the week. There were also lessons in Sumo wrestling and Japanese wooden sword fighting called *Kendo*, among other Japanese cultural activities.

Enemy alien prisoners did not have to work against their will, but those who wanted to work could earn 10 cents per hour and up to $4 per week. Jobs ranged from hospital staff to furniture factory positions to janitors. Some prisoners even worked in the INS administration offices. Those with agricultural experience could work in the camp's orange orchard, vegetable gardens, or the surrounding agricultural fields to grow food for the camp.

Our family shopped at a central grocery store at the camp or at a canteen specifically for Japanese prisoners called the Japanese Union Store, which was filled with lots of Japanese food and delicacies. There was also a separate canteen for Germans and the German General Store, filled with favorite German food. We used a form of money that was "minted" at the Crystal City market in camp. The camp scrip was pressed paper and plastic tokens that resembled coins or poker chips. The amount allocated to each family was based on the number of family members. People could earn additional scrip by volunteering for jobs. This "money" came in colors, primarily red and green, and the plastic coins were stamped with identifying information such as "Alien Detention Station Crystal City Texas," or "Crystal City Internment Camp, Clothing Token."

Papa volunteered to take on the job of a butcher at Crystal City camp. He knew fish well but preparing meat was new to him. It was an opportunity for Papa to learn and he welcomed that. His fellow workers were mostly Germans, and they were generous in sharing their knowledge, even when the language barrier made it difficult. Papa told us that even if people had little language in common, they could still share quite a bit of information. Papa seemed to respect and enjoy the company of men he worked with. I once heard him telling Mama that the Germans had old country folktales about the badger, just like in Japan. It would have been interesting to hear the German version of the *tanuki* (badger) stories and how the clever badgers fooled people. Sadly, I never had the opportunity to meet a German storyteller who could share these stories with me.

Now that Papa was part of the family once again, Kazu seemed to transform back into the spoiled princess that she was before the incarceration—at least, that was my opinion. She had no regrets handing the responsibilities of the family back to Papa. Apparently, radios were no longer considered contraband for prisoners in the camps so Kazu seemed to always be listening to the radio. Only Kazu would recall that during our time at Crystal City there were no dances for teenagers. It seems the Japanese Peruvian inmates were opposed to dances, so out of respect for their ways, dances were banned in the camp.

Mama was like an entirely new person after Papa joined us at Crystal City. She even walked with a bounce

PHOTO: NAKAGAWA PRIVATE COLLECTION

Mako pretending to be the Lone Ranger in Crystal City. Papa starred as the front of the horse with Mako sitting on his shoulders.

after our family was reunited. The weak, worried, distrusting mother was gone, and in her place was this woman who smiled a lot, even got into trying to share jokes and singing along with us—off key, as usual. Mama was much less shy socializing with the Japanese Peruvian women, and generally, just seemed happier and more relaxed.

I recall that all of us in the family flourished in this new camp. Papa would load up our homemade cart with vegetables harvested from our garden and the two of us would go past other people's living quarters, announcing we had vegetables for anyone who wanted them. Before we took off on our vegetable tour, Mama often selected the best vegetables and saved them for our Peruvian neighbors. Even my sisters noticed that Mama treated the Peruvian women with special care.

One day, we were visiting on a Peruvian woman's porch when a fire burst from a large wicker basket. A couple of the small children screamed in fear and some stared in fascination. Mama picked up a broom and began hitting the flames while calling for the older girl to bring out some water. Soon, everyone was involved in putting out the fire. When the fire was finally reduced to ashes, Mama quickly praised the kids on what a good job they had done extinguishing the flames. The neighbor woman profusely thanked Mama for her part in taking care of the incident. I was so proud of my mother. I never knew she could be so commanding and kind. This was the first time I viewed Mama as a strong person and my appreciation of having her as my mother became precious.

Once our family was reunited with Papa, smiles all around seemed to be routine for us, even in the camp surrounded by barbed-wire.

CHAPTER 22

BEING SPECIAL

When I was seven years old, I promised myself that when my turn came to have babies, I would limit myself to only two children. That way, no one would have to be a middle child.

In our family, Midori was always the sweet one. From my perspective, she got away with everything because she was the "baby of the family." On the other hand, Kazu was always given special privileges because she was the oldest and the rest of us had to obey her commands. We called her *Oneesan* (older sister), which is a title indicating her station in the family.

Mama devised a unique system of calling the elder sister by title and the younger siblings by name. Then, she gave varying titles of "sister" for each of us, giving slightly more respect to the older siblings. The eldest, Kazu, was called *"Oneesan"* by the three younger sibs. Next in line, Nobu, was called *"Nesan"* by Midori and me, and I was called *"Nechan"* by only Midori. Today, each of us calls one another only by our names. One exception is that from time to time, Midori calls me *"Nechan."* Frankly, it flatters me every time Midori calls me that, and I am nostalgic for the old terms. Midori and I have a special relationship. She remembers playing with imaginary characters from my fanciful mind. Sometimes, I would even borrow the characters Kazu and Nobu played in their early days with me as the Lone Ranger saying, "Hi-ho, Silver! Away!" and "Go, Scout, go!" for Midori who played the trusty horse. We would gallop around whatever room we had. I often played the princess and Midori was my handmaiden. I even played Santa and appointed Midori to play the naughty and greedy child. Midori contends she was always relegated to a secondary role.

Being a starstruck kid, I still resented not having more attention. Nobu didn't seem to mind being left out of the limelight, but I am told I was constantly seeking attention. When my sisters and I were grown, we talked about our family dynamics and what each of us experienced. Midori told me that both Mama and Papa were very proud of my dancing talent. I felt confident that I was a good classical Japanese-style dancer, but of course, I never felt that I was as good a dancer as Kazu. My own insecurities also dictated that there was *no* way I could be as smart as Nobu, nor as cute as Midori. As a young girl, I spent many hours trying to determine how I was going to become really *special.*

I got my chance quite by accident while living at the Crystal City camp. As Papa's constant companion, I routinely sat through his sessions with a group of *shigin* singers. *Shigin* was Papa's favorite form of Japanese singing, which is highly stylized. Most *Niseis* hated *shigin* and considered it the furthest thing from enjoyable music. I think Mama thought of yodeling or country music on the same par of irritating as *Niseis* thought of *shigin*. We kids considered Papa's *shigin* much closer to the "dying cat" sound that Mama so often laughed at. So, when I belted out the one *shigin* song I had learned while patiently sitting in the practice session, it brought on hoots of derisive laughter. But when I sang the same song to Papa's *shigin* group, they marveled at my performance and insisted I be put on the program for their upcoming recital. I became the only kid on the program and even Mama came to hear me sing in public. I felt pretty special on this occasion, but the thrill fell short of what I was looking for. As it turned out, my grand singing debut was also my farewell performance.

At a Crystal City performance,
Mako, right, providing comic relief.

Years later, Midori told me she remembers the recital quite differently. She now insists that she was standing right next to me and sang along at the *shigin* club recital that day in Texas. Funny how memory of an event can be so different from one sibling to the next! After hearing Midori's version, I started to wonder, *Could it be we got a nice round of applause because Midori was so cute? Oh no!* Maybe that's why I do not recall sharing the stage with her on that day. Either way, my *shigin* singing days ended quickly.

My next chance to stand out came not long after the day of the big *shigin* recital. There was no question that this time, I was the center of the family's attention. No longer was I a sorrowful overlooked soul, but instead, I was the most important person in the eyes of my parents and sisters. My "fifteen minutes of fame" started on an ordinary hot day in Texas when Papa came home and invited me to go swimming with him. In retrospect, it's almost unbelievable that indeed, Crystal City concentration camp had a swimming pool, and was the only American concentration camp to have a pool. The inmates at Crystal City had built it with material provided by the camp administrators.

That hot summer day, I was delighted Papa suggested going to the pool, so I didn't tell him I had been swimming earlier that afternoon. Mama just smiled and didn't tell him either. I ran to put on my still damp swimsuit, but before I could put it on, I felt a sharp sting right on my "private part," but I didn't make a sound. Somehow, Mama knew something was wrong and she was immediately by my side. Suddenly, she was swinging the iron frying pan that she happened

Mako in Crystal City music class.
She is sixth from left in the front row with long hair.

to have in her hand and she pounded the floor with it. I had no idea why. There was panic in her voice and it shook me. She screamed which brought Papa running. Mama grabbed a sheet to cover my naked body as Papa put me on his back. Mama was shouting "scorpion" and "hospital." My sisters stared at me in horror. My family's frightened concern didn't faze me, but what did amaze me was that I was the sole center of attention, and in that moment, I felt very special.

Papa ran with me on his back and Mama ran alongside. I could feel Papa getting short of breath, but he continued to run without faltering. Luckily, the hospital was not too far from our duplex. The look on Mama's face was tragic. She later confessed she was fearful the hospital would be woefully inadequate to treat something as serious as a scorpion sting. In her opinion, the word hospital was a fancy word for the facility that was barely better than a first aid station.

Later, Mama told me she wished that she could have taken me to a "real" hospital so I would have gotten the quality care she anticipated I needed.

Soon, there was going to be a big letdown. The panicked attention was about to end. The hospital staff did indeed find the spot where the scorpion stung me and medicated it. They told Mama to teach me to be cautious of damp places where scorpions were likely to hide. They also showed her how to apply the cream on my injury for the next few days. And that was the end of my hospital visit—no fuss, no bother—all over in about ten minutes. I was stunned and disappointed. "Is that all?" I asked.

To make matters even worse, another little girl was brought in with an ant bite. There was a huge commotion over her situation. Even Papa commented on the difference in staff reaction to this girl's ant bite and his daughter's scorpion sting. One staff member simply informed my father that a red ant bite could be very serious. While I was the center of attention for awhile, I never got to bask in the "glory" of surviving a scorpion sting. Besides the rather casual response of the hospital staff, I was much too embarrassed to admit to the location of the sting. To this day, I am the only one in the family with a history of being stung by a scorpion. I thought, *Along with my birthday, there should be a day to mark this momentous occasion, too. After all, I did survive!*

In later life, when I have shared my concentration camp experiences at various schools and other functions, people react to my having been a child prisoner in American concentration camps for four years, and that fact alone makes me "special" in their eyes. There were many children in the camps with me during those four years, so the last thing on my mind as a child was that one day in the future people would look on my imprisonment experience as "special." For me, my special experience was with the scorpion.

I learned much later that not all types of scorpions are deadly, and the Crystal City camp hospital treated my medical needs quite professionally. Unfortunately, it was not the job of the hospital staff to make me feel special that day. Still, I would have to find that special-ness somewhere else.

I'm special now. It took years to know this about myself, but now I know. I secretly try to help others recognize the special qualities they each possess.

And, oh yes, I broke my promise. I did give birth to more than two children. Luckily, my middle child, Bradly, didn't feel he missed out on attention that was due him—at least I think so.

CHAPTER 23

MYSTERIOUS PEOPLE

As a child, I was immersed in Japanese lifestyle and culture most of the time with only rare exposure to those who looked different than me. In our family, we ate both Japanese food and American food, but we all seemed to prefer the Japanese meals. Now that we were no longer forced to eat in the mess hall, we had the luxury of choosing our meals. We spoke English among our siblings and friends, as well as in American school or at school events. Speaking English with white people was generally rare and more of an official nature. Sometimes there was a friendly greeting. Many *Nisei* prisoners were proficient as bilingual speakers and many families counted on their children as translators when dealing with the camp authorities.

As a second grader in the concentration camp school, I was first exposed to the idea of a black person when my teacher read *Little Black Sambo* to our class. I was intrigued since I rarely had seen a black person, or for that matter, any non-Japanese people. Aside from a scattering of white people who seemed to be distant from real people, this was my first introduction to people who were different from me and from a different part of the world. Strangely, I never connected the few black people I saw in movies, radio, and cartoons as part of the same category as the East Indian character Sambo. This book was first written in 1899 and originally depicted black people in a positive light, although subsequent versions of this story were often stereotypical and considered racist.

When I first heard the story of Sambo I was captivated with the idea of Sambo getting the tigers to run around a tree and turn into butter. I thought this was fantastic. The characters in *Little Black Sambo* were a group I never knew existed, and they piqued my interest and expanded my fantasy world.

The teacher explained to us that the story was from the author's imagination. I wondered if the black people illustrated in the book with huge eyes and jet-black skin were part of that imagination, along with the transformation of tigers into butter. My exposure to different people and different cultures was very limited, especially growing up in the American concentration camps. Years later, my specialty as a professional multicultural educator might have been launched from this resoundingly discredited book.

In my own vivid imagination, I mixed the story of *Little Black Sambo* with *Gulliver's Travels* and the tiny people, the Lilliputians, who first captured Gulliver. I don't remember anyone ever reading *Gulliver's Travels* to me, but I do remember staring at the illustration of poor Gulliver tied down on the beach, a captive of the little people. I fancied myself as a friend to a whole community of black people six inches tall, like in the tale of Gulliver. I enjoyed putting Gulliver, Sambo, and myself in situations where I had an enormous ability to provide adventure in many mythical situations.

In one of my fantasies, these little people were very friendly with me. They loved to hear me sing, so when I sang they all gathered together and cheered me on. The imaginary children loved clinging to my fingers and screamed with delight as I pulled them through the air with my hands. The imaginary adult Lilliputians worked very hard to make my favorite food in large quantities for me to eat.

Of course, I was the benevolent hero in my stories. My rich fantasy life brought me great joy and refuge from my childhood in the camps. At the time, I would have been dumbfounded if anyone had pointed out the racial nuance of this fantasy.

My childhood interest in people who were different from me inspired my imaginary world. My fanciful view of Sambo was far from accurate in real life.

In addition to having no idea about the real lives of non-Japanese people, I wasn't even sure whom to ask. My knowledge of white people was limited but based on slightly more practical information. My teachers and the guards at the camps were white. Magazines and films were filled with white people. We had a name for their group; they were *hakujin* (white people), while we Japanese were *nihonjin*. Whatever term we used to show our respect, even to us young kids, it was apparent that the *hakujin* were the folks with power. From early on, we were taught to be wary of "them"—but I hardly think I was alone in being curious about "them."

One day in the second grade, my classmates and I were overcome with laughter as we took turns pressing our lips to the backs of our hands and blowing hard, making farting sounds, or in Japanese, *onara*. Each sound we produced resulted in another fresh round of hilarity. Every kid made a different sound, but each one was another variation of *onara*. We knew if the adults caught us they would disapprove, which made the humor even more delicious. What fun to be naughty!

There must have been at least a dozen of us kids trying to make the most obnoxious *onara* sound we could and commenting on one another's sounds. Then, my friend Akira produced a sound that was, hands down, the most interesting of all. He had pressed a leaf between the palms of his hands and blew into his nearly closed hands. Somehow, the vibrating leaf produced a warbling sound that was simply perfect. He drew uproarious laughter. Some of the kids even rolled around on the hard-packed dirt ground as they laughed.

I liked Akira. I was happy to see a number of the boys begging him to share his trick. He glanced at me with a smile as he revealed his secret with the waiting boys.

About this time, someone voiced a question that started a long discussion. "Why is it *hakujins* don't *onara?*"

There was lots of conjecture; half of us thought that white people did fart and the other half thought that they didn't. "They're human, they must do it," one girl insisted.

I argued that if they did do it, they would have to have a name for it. Since none of us knew the English word for *onara,* it must mean they didn't do it. Sadly, there were no *hakujins* we could ask. The only white people we had direct contact with at the camps were teachers, and sometimes military guards. We surely couldn't ask them the English word for *onara.*

My best friend, Janet, said she thought she heard one *onara* coming from her teacher. It was not conclusive because the teacher moved her chair at the same time. This teacher was either very clever in using the chair to cover her embarrassing sound, or the chair made the sound.

I knew *hakujins* were different from us, but it seemed strange to me that there was no English word for *onara.* It also seemed strange that white people's bodies would function differently from ours. I asked Mama what she thought. She just smiled and said she had no idea because she hadn't been around *hakujins* very much. She implied she wouldn't want to know them well enough to answer my question.

One day when I was alone with Janet, the subject came up again. We finally came to the conclusion that the only logical explanation was as follows: *onara* was the result of what one ate. Since *hakujins* ate differently from us, it made sense their food simply did not produce *onara.*

I never learned how to eat non-*onara* producing *hakujin* food as I had once planned. However, as time went by, I did learn some English words for *onara*, such as "fart," "passing gas," "cut the cheese," and "flatulence." *Ah Ha! They did do it after all! One more mystery about white people solved!* I thought.

Slowly, but surely, I was learning we are not so different from one another after all.

CHAPTER 24

INSIDE OR OUTSIDE?

One day a group of kids was mesmerized by the demise of a huge rat that our neighbor had captured and killed. We were gathered in the vegetable garden behind his living quarters, next to ours. Because I was in charge of watching my four-year-old sister, I made sure she didn't get too close to the dead rat. It looked menacing, even when dead.

The neighbor was busy talking to several adults, giving them a blow-by-blow account of how he killed the rat. They weren't paying attention to the children, so I ventured closer to the rat in morbid fascination, keeping Midori well behind me. The neighbor sauntered over, picked the rat up by its tail, and swung it in several complete circles above his head. Finally, he flung the rat way over the barbed-wire fence and far into the desert.

I don't think Superman himself could have looked more courageous and dashing than my neighbor at that moment. Until then, I never knew such bravery existed. I know his heroics also impressed Midori because she let out a loud "Wow!"

We rushed back to our quarters to tell Mama of our adventure. Luckily, Midori was out of breath so I got to be first to tell the story. Midori quickly recovered and took over. Mama seemed duly impressed and commented that our neighbor was indeed a brave man.

That evening, I overheard Mama telling Papa about our amazing outing. She told him how excited Midori and I were in relaying the story to her, especially the part about how impressed we were with our brave neighbor. But strangely, she then chose to focus on neither the rat nor on our hero neighbor but on the last sentence of my sister's version of the story.

My sister had mistakenly told Mama that the rat was flung far *inside* the fence. Of course, I knew the rat was actually flung far outside the fence and had told Mama so. Mama seemed perturbed over Midori's mistake and I wondered why. Why would the one wrong word disturb Mama so? I wondered, *What's the big deal on whether we were inside the fence or outside the fence?*

Mama slowly shook her head repeating "inside the fence. Oh my…." Papa looked a little sad, too. I didn't resolve the mystery of this conversation until years later when I was watching a movie on TV where a man is just let out of prison. He kept saying, "I'm on the outside! I'm on the outside! I'm free! I'm free!"

I finally made the connection.

CHAPTER 25

GOING HOME

The news of the war ending reached us while we were in Crystal City camp. On September 2, 1945, Japan surrendered to the United States. There was much commotion among all of the prisoners in reaction to this news. Even though I was young, I knew this was big news and people were very happy.

Not long after the end of the war, U.S. families slowly began leaving the camp, including hundreds of Japanese returning to Hawaii. Hundreds of Germans returned to Germany, and in December 1945 some 600 Peruvian Japanese left for Japan because their own country, Peru, would not accept them back. However, hundreds of Peruvian Japanese prisoners refused to participate in the U.S. repatriation program back to Japan. They were not allowed to return to Central or South America, so more than 300 Peruvian Japanese filed a lawsuit to stay in the United States. In late 1947, the U.S. government finally agreed to let the Peruvian Japanese stay in the United States. The Crystal City concentration camp officially closed down on February 11, 1948, becoming the last camp detaining enemy aliens.

We did not leave Crystal City until late April 1946. Our imprisonment at this camp had lasted two years, which made our family's incarceration time in American concentration camps a total of four years and one month. For Papa, it had been even longer. A life on the outside as free people was about to begin for us.

In retrospect, it seems the reason we were among the last families to leave the camp was partly due to the prolonged disagreement between my parents. Mama and Papa had nightly arguments. They would put us to bed and then argue loudly about the best course of action. Mama was very much in favor of returning to Japan. She was sure that Japan was the only place we would be given fair treatment. Papa had misgivings about returning to a war-torn country. He was worried about getting a job and having enough money. We heard that things in Japan were really bad after the war. Their arguments persisted until Papa asked Kazu, who was now 15, what her vote would be. She said, "Seattle," and Mama accepted it.

My report card from the Crystal City school in Texas listed me as "Masako," which is my legal name, and noted my withdrawing from school on April 5, 1946. Though the majority of people had left Crystal City before us, there were still people left behind the day we departed, such as the Peruvian Japanese who refused to repatriate to Japan.

While I was focused on just getting out of the camp, I am sure my parents worried about starting a new life again in Seattle. I did have my own ideas of what I might encounter when we got back to Seattle. I remember preparing for our departure from Crystal City by asking friends to sign my autograph book. More than 70 years later, I still have that autograph book although I hardly recognize any of the names. One person even drew a flattering sketch of me in my book. In addition to my autograph book, few things survived the many years since our incarceration experience. To this day, I still have the following items: My school report card, a few photos, one textbook from our Japanese class, and plastic coins that had been camp scrip.

These few mementos represent four years of my childhood in the camps. Several years after my family had resettled in Seattle, I once brought a few plastic camp coins to school when it was my turn to share stories from my past. After my "show and tell," the teacher insisted that my story was not correct because my family had lived in Texas, which is part of the United States, and the plastic "money" I shared was not the same as the money we used in the U.S. Puzzled, the teacher examined the coins to prove they were not legitimate U.S. currency. She gave the coins back to me and said nothing more. Clearly, she knew nothing about my experience in a concentration camp during the war.

I don't know what happened to those coins and sometimes I wonder why I would even want them today. However, I admit that if I had those coins today, I would definitely hold on to them because they had been a part of my childhood.

Preparing to leave Crystal City included packing the essentials, giving away things that might be handy for those still remaining in the camp and tossing some items we did not want to carry on the long trip home. My parents filled out the required paperwork to depart, and I think we got $25 for each family member and tickets for the train ride to Seattle. Much later, Papa told me he didn't receive the money, so it is possible we were overlooked.

My family sought out any news accounts of anti-Japanese activity from those who had left the camp earlier. My parents wanted to know about white people's attitudes and treatment of Japanese Americans. We all wondered, *Will they resent our return to the Seattle area?*

We cringed at some of the harsh negative stories but strived to remain positive as best we could. My parents would often try to comfort each other and us kids by saying, "It can't be that bad. America is a good country."

Many stories from former prisoners included being called "Japs," even in the news media. Japanese Americans were often ignored when seeking service at stores, restaurants, and gas stations. There were even stories of angry people spitting on Japanese Americans or heckling and threatening them. We children heard bits of stories about Japanese students being harassed at school, and sometimes, the Japanese students feared for their own safety. Stories from outside the camps became more numerous. Some of the stories confirmed by news articles were outright frightening.

We were ready to go "home," but we questioned how "home" would react to us. The persistent question was, "How will we be treated when we return home?"

At nine years old, I remember some parts of preparing to leave Crystal City, but the strange thing is I don't remember any part of the actual trip back to Seattle. Why is the trip back to Seattle a complete void in my mind? There was nothing about it that was traumatic. However, both of my older sisters have some memories of our trip back. Their recollections were pretty reasonable under the circumstances.

Kazu told me the train was a newer version of the rickety, worn-down ones that took us from one camp to another. Kazu said she enjoyed being free and being able to keep the window shades open while on the train. The ride home was far different than the ride to the camps where military guards watched our every move. Kazu said she almost made the mistake of raising her hand on the ride home, forgetting she no longer had to ask for permission to use the restroom. Luckily, no one noticed her. Kazu had to remind herself, *I am free—free to move about the train and even go to the dining car and order our meals.*

Nobu remembers parts of the train ride home, in particular, seeing the reflection of a cute soldier in a train glass; he was not a guard but just a fellow passenger. Nobu stared at his reflection thinking he would not notice her stare. At one point, he even walked back to where she was sitting and conversed with her. At twelve years old, Nobu thinks that might have constituted her first flirtation episode.

Once we arrived back home, I had almost no recollection of Seattle after being away for four years. I did remember the house we rented in 1942 and I would have liked to revisit that house to confirm my recollections, but it was no longer available to us. We had to start over and find a new place to live.

At first, we moved into a small apartment that already housed a family of five. We had met these friends in the Crystal City concentration camp and when we returned to Seattle, they were very generous to invite us to stay with them. However, with six in our family and five in theirs, it was quickly apparent that we needed to find our own lodging. With the help of our Buddhist minister, Reverend Ichikawa, who was also a former prisoner at Crystal City camp, we found a place to live with reasonable rent. Many others returning to Seattle were herded into public housing, church gymnasiums, and makeshift mobile units, so in many ways, our family was fortunate.

Employment was much harder to secure even when Papa was not being picky. After a prolonged search, Papa was offered a job as an orderly at Providence Hospital. The pay for the job was painfully low to support a family of six. Yet, Papa was about ready to accept this job because he was feeling desperate. However, a few of Papa's friends met with him and discouraged him from accepting this job. Their reasoning was that such an employment downgrade, especially after Papa's previous experience in a managerial position, and as a leader in the community prior to the war, would have an adverse effect on all the others seeking work. In order to avoid this dramatic cut in pay and employment responsibility, Papa's friends pooled their money and asked Papa to manage a small grocery store they had just bought. Papa accepted.

For years after the war, Papa, along with most of the *Nikkei* people, barely subsisted after they returned home. It took awhile before better employment opportunities slowly became available. Surprisingly, it was the government itself that opened doors to potential Japanese American workers.

Mama was primarily a busy housewife with four young children prior to the war, but she did have a brief span of time working as a certificated barber. She managed to purchase a barber's chair and had plans to open a barbershop to help make money for the family. This idea never came to fruition but we children had fun playing on the big chair.

In addition to working as a store manager, Papa was resourceful in figuring out other ways to support his family. He started a bean sprout business, at first selling to restaurants, but eventually expanding his sales to various food markets. This was a new concept and Papa gave it a go. I remember watching my father nourish the sprout seeds, and when ready, package them and deliver to his customers. Papa also got involved in the Japanese movie business, distributing films in the Japanese community. For many years, Papa used his California contacts to route Japanese movies to various entertainment venues in the Japanese community. My family often previewed these movies at home, using our refrigerator as a screen. We learned a lot about Japanese culture just by watching these imported movies.

Even though Papa involved himself in a number of enterprises, he was never able to regain the stature he had attained prior to the war. Papa did what he could and was grateful for all the support his daughters provided him. Even though Papa's economic gains were meager, I think Papa, as well as the rest of the family, was sure that he made the right decision to return to Seattle rather than return to Japan. The United States was our home.

Just when it looked like things were improving, Papa got word that his mother had passed away. Papa had a special place in his heart for old folks and for kids. He was very partial to his mother even though he had not seen her since he left Japan at 19 years old. We had always gotten the impression that Papa was a favorite son out of four sons and he had a special connection with his mom. More than three decades had passed and Papa hadn't been back to Japan to see his mother. Frequently, Papa told us stories about his mother but we never got to meet our *obaasan*.

In his grief, and perhaps regret, Papa did comment that had we left camp to go to Japan, he would have had at least one occasion to see his mother before she died. We felt sorrow for our father but since none of us had ever met his mother, it was difficult to comfort him. We each tried to listen to Papa talk while he mourned but we each felt sorry we could not validate our loss and share his sadness. We just gave him all the love we could—that was all we knew to do.

CHAPTER 26

BACK TO SCHOOL IN SEATTLE

Getting resettled in Seattle mostly meant settling into school. One of the first things I noticed when I returned to our local grammar school was that the classrooms were exceedingly well furnished compared to the classrooms in the concentration camps. As for the students, I immediately noticed that the students were not predominately Japanese American like me. There were only three *Nikkei* students in my new class, but we seemed to be a racially diverse group, including black, white, and Hispanic students. We were also diverse in terms of religion, income levels, and culture.

One of my goals was to be friends with kids who were different than me, especially black students. One group that completely perplexed me was the students who called themselves Jewish. I had never encountered this group before. They looked *hakujin* (white), but seemed to be less privileged than other whites. At nine years old, I didn't have the slightest idea of how they had been persecuted during the war, but I did sense that they were treated differently. One thing I admired is how Jewish students were excused from school on certain days as part of their religion, and I liked that idea.

It was at recess time when other kids openly challenged us Japanese American kids by demanding to know which "race" we were. In those days, the question usually was "Are you Japanese or Chinese?"

I knew I wanted to say I was Chinese just so I could avoid the ugly gestures after I admitted I was Japanese, but that would have been a lie. Papa encouraged us to be proud of our Japanese heritage but in school I wasn't proud to be Japanese. Quietly I would answer "Japanese" and inevitably their nasty gestures followed. Maybe they'd stick a finger into their mouths, posing to aim for the throat, and acting as if they would vomit. Or maybe they'd pull the corners of their eyes to make fun of our looks or just plain snicker at us. Some kids were obnoxious enough to come up to me and announce that their mothers had told them "not to play with Japs."

Around this time in my life, I began to long to be white. I was too ashamed to openly admit this longing for whiteness, but it was true. I wanted to be white because only white people seemed to escape the taunting. There seemed to be no limitations on what the white kids could do or be. I used to think, *If I were white, I could be a movie star like the child actors Shirley Temple or Margaret O'Brian. What would stop me from becoming anything I wanted if I were white?*

I knew that with my appearance, I could never become the Queen of Hearts. Secretly, I suffered my lonely longing, never telling anyone that I wallowed in my desire to be white. Often, I wondered, *Why is being*

Japanese so bad? What did the Japanese do that made other people hate us so much?

Whatever it was, many people did seem to hate us. In turn, for the pain they caused me, I was mad at them, too. Nobu taught me to quit acquiescing to ignorant classmates. When someone asked me, "Are you Japanese?" Nobu taught me to respond with, "I'm an American."

I tried Nobu's suggestion a number of times, but it did not work too often. So, I went from faulting the Japanese for *their* wrongdoing—of which I knew nothing—to blaming other nonwhite kids. When a nonwhite kid said something mean to me, I thought, *They are not white, so they should be on my side.*

Mako, age 10, with Santa Claus.

Then I decided to hold the white kids as the culprit. I held the U.S. government responsible for the meanness around me—I figured the people in the government were all white. Over a long period of time, I seemed to have held everyone guilty for causing me so much turmoil and pain.

At the very same time I was going through faulting all these people, I would join other Japanese American

202

kids and shout out deplorable things to put other kids down. We'd shout back mean names at other groups and laugh at them. We even criticized the rich kids, although we mostly envied them.

I am amazed at how quickly I picked up these hurtful words which were mostly unknown to me when my family was incarcerated in the camps. To make matters worse, I learned spiteful attitudes toward groups of people solely based on society's judgments and pecking order. Racial name calling on the playground was routine and no adult intervened to stop our hurtful words and behaviors. It took me a long time to figure out what was right.

There were three occasions during my elementary school years in Seattle when I took action and tried to stand my ground with school faculty. These were the first glimmerings of me learning to stand up for myself in the face of authority figures—teachers and parents.

The first time involved the only boy in my class who was of Japanese ancestry. He was very cute and I often watched him carefully as he performed his duties as a patrol boy. Girls were not allowed to become patrol girls and I wanted to change that so I could spend more time with the patrol boy I liked. I carefully set a time to talk to the teacher about allowing me to join the patrol. I asserted that girls would be just as responsible in performing patrol duties and just needed an opportunity to show how well they could work. I was afraid the teacher would simply pat me on the head with some platitude, but this was not the case.

She promised to bring my idea up at the faculty meeting. I was all geared up to make my pitch to the faculty, but the decision had come down and my proposal was turned down. The teacher commended me for the "excellent" idea. Though I wished it had been approved, I was actually proud I made the suggestion and that the faculty considered my idea. I felt I did something notable, even when my main motivation was just to get better acquainted with that one boy!

The second time I confronted an authority figure was with a different teacher. We had read the poem by Robert Louis Stevenson "Foreign Children," and we were required to memorize it. Some parts of the poem I did not like, especially the last two stanzas, and I didn't want to memorize them. They read:

> *You have curious things to eat,*
> *I am fed on proper meat;*
> *You must dwell beyond the foam,*
> *But I am safe and live at home.*
>
> *Little Indian, Sioux or Crow,*
> *Little frosty Eskimo,*
> *Little Turk or Japanee*
> *O! don't you wish that you were me?*

I worried that my objection to this poem might offend the teacher, but the sentiments of this poem were very bothersome. My whole body was shaking when I walked up to the teacher to express my concerns. I did not like the way Stevenson referred to Japanese as "Japanee." It felt like a put down. I don't remember what I said to her, but I do recall her response to me. "Oh, that's okay, Masako dear because you're an American now."

Her response was hurtful. I felt completely misunderstood.

The third incident was the biggest move I had made at that point in my life and potentially the most devastating one. When Mama and I went to the school to register me, the office attendant and I assumed I would be enrolled in the fourth grade. Mama had me translate for her and tell the office attendant that she thought I should be placed in the third grade. Earlier before we visited the school, Mama did suggest to me that I should repeat the third grade, but I didn't think she was serious. At the school, she explained to the office attendant that the camp schools were inferior, and she wanted me to have a good foundation for learning.

I was horrified but felt compelled to translate Mama's words faithfully. I was convinced that Mama was more concerned with my scholastic ability rather than the quality of schools in the camps. It felt like I wore a big "D" on my forehead to announce to the world that I was a "dummy." For a whole school year I cringed every day as I sat amongst the third graders. At the end of that year, I approached my teacher and expressed to her my desire to skip the fourth grade and be promoted into the fifth grade. I assured the teacher that I would be able to keep pace with the fifth graders and would work extra hard to make sure I stayed true to my word.

Later, I overheard my teacher speaking to the principal regarding my potential promotion, but I couldn't make out her specific words. I saw him look like he was asking questions and then I saw him nodding "yes." Suddenly, I felt tremendous relief at the thought that I would regain my place with my age group in the fifth grade. But right after my relief followed more anxiety. *How do I tell Mama?*

It took all my courage to ask my teacher for what I wanted. Now, I wondered, *Where do I find the courage and boldness to face Mama with the truth of what I just did? How do I weather the storm that is sure to follow?*

As a brave young girl, I thought about this for weeks but did nothing. The summer came and went and still, Mama was thinking I was going to be a fourth grader. I started school as a fifth grader and Mama still was not apprised of the situation. The close of the first quarter of school was recorded with the first quarter report cards. After Papa signed the report card, Mama looked at my report card carefully and then pointed to the grade assignment and simply asked, "Is this a mistake?"

Mama couldn't read English but she sure could read numbers and deduced the number signified my grade level. I mumbled, "No, it isn't a mistake." Then I told her the teachers thought I was ready for the fifth grade and they made the promotion. Mama smiled and said, "That's nice," and that was that. Holy Smoke! I felt I had just been spared from the guillotine.

In retrospect, there were a number of times that things went smoothly because we clearly accepted that we were not white, and we were the outsiders. I think all the nonwhite students accepted this reality and we just learned to live in the white world. We understood its norms and rules. For instance, when our teacher asked

Mako, right, at about thirteen years old, and Midori.

the Japanese students what we had for breakfast, we made up an "acceptable" menu like cereal or pancakes, rather than admit we had raw fish, pickles, and egg rice with salmon eggs. We intuitively understood that would be more than the white teachers could handle.

For the most part, the teachers and administrators at our school, all white, did well or meant well. However, there were those occasions when cultural differences or cultural ignorance on their part was downright laughable. Sometimes, I just thought white people were strange because I didn't understand why they did or said certain things.

For instance, Midori was apparently fidgety in class and she had difficulty staying in her assigned seat. She was only in kindergarten, but back then the teachers expected the youngsters to sit still in their

PHOTO: NAKAGAWA PRIVATE COLLECTION

Mako performing a traditional Japanese dance in her early teens.

seats. One day, Midori's teacher pulled me aside and suggested that I ask my mother to not include the "huge coconut balls" in Midori's lunch because that might be the source of her sugar high. *Huge coconut balls?* I didn't know what she meant, but I nodded in agreement that I would talk to Mama. It took me a little while to figure out what the teacher saw in Midori's lunch. Those were rice balls not coconut balls!

One of my grammar school teachers recognized that I spoke Japanese fairly well. She urged me to keep up my use of the language. She predicted, "People with multilingual skills will be of much value in the future." Then again, another one of my teachers insisted that I learn to use spoons and forks so that people would not laugh at me when I used chopsticks. She admonished, "If you want people to truly think of you as American and not as a foreigner, then use American utensils."

I thought these two incidents were somewhat humorous, but I did start thinking, *Who should decide what Japanese things I should keep and what Japanese things I should toss?*

This question troubled me at my young age. This really became a lifetime question of where to assimilate into the "white American" culture and where to hold onto my Japanese identity and traditions. This included when to speak honestly and when to hide my true feelings.

One incident in particular brought home my frustration and conflicted feelings about being Japanese American in a post World War II America. I was in the fifth grade when the head librarian at the local public library asked me how I would rate the camp experience. "Was it poor or was it good?" she asked in front of her fellow librarians.

I quickly assured her it was "very good," believing this was the "right" answer she wanted from me. The librarian quickly turned to her assistant and seemed to gloat because she had gotten the answer she had predicted from me. She went on to tell the assistant, "The 'smart ones' knew they were being protected."

When I heard her say this, I felt cheated. I expected her to note what a polite, upbeat, and respectful young lady I was. Instead, the librarian gloated over being right. Silently, I told myself, *Mama would approve of my response to the librarian's question.*

There would be many times when I just thought, *White people sure can be strange sometimes.*

CHAPTER 27

I PLEDGE ALLEGIANCE—TO WHAT?

While living behind the barbed-wire fences as a child prisoner, I had to learn and recite the Pledge of Allegiance. At the time I first learned the Pledge, Papa was imprisoned in a separate camp from ours, and we had no idea if we would ever see Papa again or when we would be free. Several months earlier, the FBI had taken Papa to an undisclosed place, and we didn't even know *why* he had been taken.

There I was, a five-year-old inmate with her hand over her heart reciting "...with liberty and justice for all."

In truth, I learned to mimic a few sounds of words that are in the Pledge of Allegiance without learning the meaning of the words. I didn't know what a "pledge" was nor did I know how to pronounce many of the other words. Two of the words were especially difficult—indivisible and allegiance. I remember saying "indivisible" and "allegiance" over and over again trying to pronounce these strange words.

Nobu tried to explain the word "indivisible" to me by taking pieces of candy from one candy bar. I saw no connection, but I nodded in agreement when she asked if I understood. My tactic of bringing the boring lesson to a close was effective. It seems this was the only lesson anyone ever attempted in order to help me understand the words in the Pledge of Allegiance.

As a teenager in the 1950s, the Pledge became a wonderful American promise that allowed me a comfortable sense of belonging and of patriotic pride. I am loathe to admit that I also felt a tinge of smugness. I swelled with tearful pride and abject loyalty just watching the American flag pass by.

About this time, I became involved in the controversy over the proposal to add two more words to the Pledge. I was passionately opposed to the addition of "under God," which was added in 1954. I argued in class, as well as with individuals, expressing my opposition. I did not consider myself an atheist, but the thought of excluding atheists by adding these two words seemed un-American and wrong in my opinion. To me, freedom of religion meant that one always had the option to not have a religion.

This was the beginning of my politicization as a young adult. I was sorely disappointed that the addition to the Pledge was accepted. I vowed to never utter those added words, "under God," when I recited the Pledge.

Later, I began questioning the validity of the Pledge as a symbol of inalienable rights and unwavering principles of American democracy. I wondered if the teachers from my early youth who taught us the Pledge in the camp schools understood the irony of teaching us

the Pledge of Allegiance while our own country imprisoned us. I wondered, *Did they teach by rote, just as I was
expected to learn by rote? Or were they shaken by the
inherent contradictions between the governmental words
and governmental action?*

It would be many years before I understood the full
implications of this Pledge in my life.

After I began questioning the Pledge of Allegiance
as a symbol of inalienable rights and unwavering principles of American democracy, I got caught up in the
mood of the 1960s to challenge the status quo and the
authorities. I developed a swagger along with my growing assertiveness of Japanese American rights. Borrow-
ing from the Black community, I was shouting, "Yellow
is Beautiful!"

I decried my childhood learning of the Pledge as "hy-
pocrisy in action."

After I became a mother of three by the 1970s,
my political outlook shifted dramatically. I put aside
protest posters and my outrage, and I turned my attention to pressing parenting questions of daily life. "Should

Daren be allowed another cookie before dinner?" "Does DeeAn's diaper rash need a doctor's attention?" "Does Bradly need new shoes?"

Thoughts of the Pledge of Allegiance were far removed from my family life with three young children in tow. However, later in the decade when my children were in school, I realized that they were affected by the society around them. I thought, *Perhaps I should consider social activism again.*

Soon, the Pledge was back in my life as I began my teaching profession. My day with second grade students began with the Pledge of Allegiance. As I fumbled with all the challenges facing me as a new teacher, the Pledge was simply a rote part of the morning routine. In time, it was most humbling and disheartening to realize that I had become part of the problem and not part of the solution. In hindsight, I considered, *Maybe my teachers in the concentration camps were just like me—simply overwhelmed teachers.*

In the 1980s, I became a principal at a Seattle elementary school. Whenever possible, I went from classroom to classroom during the morning routine, which included the Pledge of Allegiance. I was careful to silently mouth the words "under God," intent on setting a proper example for the students but also unwilling to voice out loud those two specific words. I continued to silently object to those words that I felt hurt all of us.

It often struck me as remarkable that I was an adult model at school teaching the Pledge, yet personally so painfully conflicted. However, I did make it a point to encourage the teachers to discuss the meaning of the

Pledge with their students. Neither the students nor the teachers were aware of the circumstances under which I first learned the Pledge.

By the 1990s, my personal and professional lives profoundly changed. The only time I can recall even reciting the Pledge was at the opening of a few Mariner baseball games I attended. By the end of the decade, I was partially retired and looking forward to enjoying more leisure time. I planned to indulge in "mindless entertainment," which I felt I deserved. The talent, skills, knowledge, and self-confidence of the younger generation comforted me, and I decided, *I will leave it to them to address the social issues of the day and of the future.*

Once again, the Pledge had receded to the far recesses of my awareness. I was intent on relishing the joys and leisure of retirement. However, life has a way of turning good intentions upside down. Little did I know what the new millenium would bring.

CHAPTER 28

House Girls & Care Packages

The worst part of Mama and Papa's financial worries occurred during their resettlement in Seattle in the late 1940s. In my opinion, my parents endured hardships even more severe than during the Great Depression in the 1930s. Mama's idea to set up a barbershop and cut hair again was beyond her capabilities. Her days were full taking care of her growing family.

Papa's job offers were rare, temporary, and hardly adequate to provide for the family. Like many *Nikkei* families, Mama and Papa counted on the help of their kids to make ends meet. Paper routes, summer fruit and vegetable harvesting, babysitting, and waitressing, among other odd jobs for young people, helped bring in some of the needed money for the family.

At one time or another during our high school years, each of us lived with a prosperous white family and worked as a "house girl." We remained in school and we were paid a modest sum in addition to being housed with the family. Our chores as house girls included washing the dishes, ironing clothes, dusting, polishing silver, babysitting, and serving the evening meal to the family.

Mako, second from right, at
her junior high school in Seattle, 1952.

In addition to a modest wage, this "house girl" job also gave our own family one less mouth to feed.

The family I stayed with provided a tiny room that was the finest room I had ever had as my bedroom. The house was located across the street from the gated residential community, Broadmoor, where only whites could buy homes. The luxury everywhere in the house was shouting to me, "You don't belong here!"

It felt wrong that my family felt so happy to have one toilet for eleven of us while incarcerated at the Crystal City camp, but as a "house girl" in Seattle I had one toilet and a shower for just me. The family was quite nice and the kids were most curious about me, but I still had the feeling, "You don't belong here!"

The white family I worked for ate in the dining room and I ate in the kitchen. The mistress had a small bell which she rang if she needed something. If the bell rang, I rushed into the dining room and the mistress would tell me what necessary task I needed to handle. As a teenager, I could not articulate *why* this responsibility was the one that made me feel, "You don't belong here!" the strongest. I disliked being a house girl and never thought I would call it a good experience, but strangely, it was. When I got older, I concluded I needed to learn and grow from bad experiences as well as good ones. At the time, it was my attitude that caused the self-inflicted wounds. In time, I learned I could become strong enough to terminate an unfortunate understanding without faulting anyone unnecessarily. I was learning to be more like an adult.

During that same time, Mama and Papa were diligently preparing relief packages for relatives in Japan. I barely took notice of the activity. It was difficult to even imagine any relative worse off than we were at the time, but my parents were worried about family starving in post-World War II Japan. I don't know if the people in Japan really ate rats as we had heard, but I knew we shared our house in Seattle with big rats. I longed for a house without rats and wondered when that paradise would come to pass. I mostly ignored my parents' bustle of CARE packaging.

CARE, which stands for Cooperative for American Remittances to Europe, began in 1946 to help Europeans struggling to survive after WW II. That relief was soon extended to Japan. Japanese Americans on the West Coast were the driving force behind this effort.

I had never met the Japanese relatives and didn't feel a bond with them. Mama had never met these relatives either, but they were Papa's kin, so she cared. Not until years later would I understand how much our Japanese relatives appreciated the CARE packages.

Japanese were truly on the brink of disaster and despair, trying to rebuild their country after the war. Decades later when I understood the desperate situation in Japan, I was so grateful that Mama and Papa sent these packages, even when they had tremendous needs in Seattle. Many *Nikkei* families were in the same shoes, struggling to get by, but they too were sending their CARE packages to Japan.

I silently resented the attention my parents gave these relatives. On occasion, I took Mama's package to the post office to send off to Japan but that was the extent of my participation. I felt generous for simply not voicing my resentment. Reflecting on those times years later, I often wonder, *Where did Mama get her motivation?*

The sense of community extending from family and the Japanese community was very strong. Many times the conversation among *Nikkei* families in our community was about what were the best things to send to Japan via CARE. They needed warm clothes, nonperishable food, and other lightweight items that might ease their suffering. They even chuckled that Vienna sausages might be appreciated. Toys for the young ones were still prized but mostly food, food, food—*that* was the prime order of the day. I have experienced poverty but I never experienced poverty to the point of constant hunger and fear of dying of starvation.

One of the items Mama frequently sent in the packages headed to Japan was Lipton's Chicken Noodle Soup. It was simple to fix—just add boiling water to the contents of the package and let it simmer for ten or so minutes. It had the advantage of being salty in flavor with good taste, minimal weight, and took up little space in a CARE package. The problem was the Japanese relatives didn't know what it was. One neighbor in Japan had a little background in English and read the label: "So" then "up." He deduced it was "soap." They tried out the package of soup out at the bathhouse but became confused and disappointed. A few months later, the relatives in Japan told us they thought it strange that the "soap" didn't foam. They put the package of soup aside and were very pleasantly surprised when one of the teenage kids took it upon herself to try cooking it. Several weeks later, it became a favorite of the clan. They regretted the wasted packages ruined at the bathhouse. It was salty, it was good, and the relatives greatly appreciated it.

Many decades after my Japanese relatives opened up these packages with childlike glee I finally met them. Years later, I visited Japan for the first time and heard their stories. It was hard to visualize that these well-dressed people in comfortable homes, generously hosting our visit to Japan, were once so desperate for even the meager items Mama and Papa sent. Most of my Japanese relatives admitted they cried with joy whenever a new shipment arrived. They cried again when they shared their stories with me. For the first time, I felt pride for my parents' efforts to reach out to their relatives in Japan, even when they were scraping by in Seattle.

When the CARE packages were no longer vital to our relatives in Japan, a group of people in Seattle initiated a drive soliciting funds to build a nursing home in Seattle, fulfilling the special needs and comforts for people of Japanese ancestry. Papa told me how proud he was to participate in such a wonderful project. Imagine having access to soy sauce right on the dining table, interpreters when doctors gave them updates, hearing pleasant Japanese music and video dramas, and of course, Japanese food. Papa was conscious of his own old age creeping up within his foreseeable future. He was living on his limited income from Social Security, but he still found a way to contribute a token sum for this effort. To the end, Papa and Mama were generous.

CHAPTER 29

A Message from Sakura

We were always in a good mood when we packed ourselves into the car to go cherry blossom or *sakura* viewing, which usually took place in late March or maybe early April for only a couple of weeks. Papa would drive along the boulevard lined with *sakura* (cherry blossom trees), and Mama would "ooh" and "aaah" over their beauty, glorious with their pink and white blossoms gently floating to earth in a light breeze. This was really Mama's outing and that was nice because she was rarely the center of our family activities. In time, this would become one of my fondest childhood memories with my family—one that would give me comfort during some of my most difficult days.

The first cherry blossom trees in Seattle were a gift from Japan in 1912 when times were good. That same year, Japan also gifted 3,000 cherry blossom trees to Washington, D.C., starting a tradition that, to this day, is an essential part of the U.S. capital's beauty. *Sakura* is Japan's national flower, along with the chrysanthemum, and its dramatic, short-lived beauty is considered a symbol for "the poetry of the Japanese soul."

In friendship, Japan gifted additional cherry blossom trees to the University of Washington in 1939 as a symbol of its ties to the school. Sadly, just four years after those trees were planted in friendship, more than 400 Japanese American students at the university were forced into U.S. concentration camps and their education disrupted. There was talk during World War II to cut down all of these cherry trees due to anger toward the Japanese. Fortunately, that didn't happen, although four cherry trees in Washington, D.C. were anonymously cut down, most likely out of spite toward the Japanese.

My family usually drove down Lake Washington Boulevard with Lake Washington on our left and well-manicured homes on the right. The street was bursting with cherry trees, one after another, flaunting their glory. We would end up at Seward Park in southeastern Seattle, surrounded by water on three sides. After picking the best place for our viewing pleasure, we placed our *gozas* (straw mats) on the ground and enjoyed our *bentos* (meals) amongst the brilliant *sakura*.

Whenever we took this traditional family ride, our praise of the *sakura* was the same, which was somehow very comforting to me as a child. We did not go every year, but when we did go, it was memorable.

One year, all six of us ate our *bento* in the cramped car because of a rainstorm. Our car was a four-door Chevrolet, but with six of us crammed into the car it was surprising how we managed to all eat. While we hungrily ate our *bentos*, Papa started laughing at how silly it was that we didn't just take the food home and eat where we had more space. We laughed with Papa, but we kept eating in the car. We could hardly see the cherry trees, but we were *with* them. I felt even more snug and cozy with my family that year among the *sakura.*

Each year that we visited the *sakura,* the food differed from *bento* to *bento* but the rice balls were always the same. It was the *hinomaru nigiri,* in English "round sun riceball," which is a red plum preserved in salt and wrapped in white rice. The rice ball with the little red sphere in the middle represented the Japanese flag. Mama's nostalgia for her early life in Japan was apparent but rarely spoken about. Sometimes, Mama talked about her childhood in Japan as our family shared *hinomaru nigiri.* It was unusual for Mama to talk about her early years in Japan, so when she did, we listened intently.

One time while I was alone with Mama preparing food for our family outing to see the *sakura,* I asked her why *sakura* was so special. "The azaleas, the rhododendrons and even the apple tree blossoms are just as beautiful as the cherry tree, Mama. Why the big fuss over *sakura?*"

Mama spoke almost no English, so she carefully chose her words and explained in Japanese. "The full bloom of *sakura* does not last very long. Their beautiful lives are very short so this makes them even more precious."

Somehow that didn't make sense to me! "If *sakura* lasted the whole week, or two weeks, or two months, how would that make the beauty any less beautiful?"

Mama shook her head and said the equivalent of "you just don't get it. You're being argumentative. Maybe when you are older...."

She was right. I didn't get it. Now that I am much older than Mama was at the time I asked her that question, I wonder, *Have I finally aged enough to have "gotten" it?*

Maybe it is not just the time spent on the planet that helped me understand what Mama meant. Maybe the intervening years and the sorrows I have experienced have helped bring Mama's joy of the *sakura* into my life.

Among my many losses, I lost Mama and Papa; I lost my long-standing marriage of 30 years through divorce; and I lost friends to disease, old age, and accidents. One relative was even murdered. I grieved deeply over each of these losses, and strangely, I found the most comfort and closure in thinking of Mama and her joy viewing the *sakura*. Maybe Mama's message was to soak up the gift of the sakura, instill that experience into your heart, and then watch the petals fall with restful resignation and acceptance.

Now, I have reached the sunset years of my life. The blossom of my life is hanging on, but the petals are beginning to scatter. My life, too, will pass, but what a fortunate person I am to have so many memories to treasure, and I have survived many hardships with my spirit intact. I think this is how Mama saw life during our *sakura* viewing days.

My life is simply one of the *sakura* blossoms swirling among others, leaving the sturdy cherry trees, drifting to ground gracefully like snowflakes in the winter. It is all part of nature's beauty and nature's way.

Now I wonder, *Mama did I finally get it?*

EPILOGUE

Righting the Injustices: Papa's Testimony

The U.S. Congress and President Jimmy Carter appointed nine people for the Commission on Wartime Relocation and Internment of Civilians (CWRIC), established in 1980. Their job was to conduct an official government study on whether wrongs had been committed in the rounding up and incarceration of Japanese Americans during World War II. The commission was charged with investigating the facts and circumstances surrounding Executive Order 9066, which allowed the U.S. government to incarcerate some 120,000 Japanese Americans. A part of the commission's work was to hold public hearings and let those directly affected by Executive Order 9066 tell their stories.

At first, I was against the process of creating a commission. My contention was that it was blatantly obvious how Japanese Americans were damaged. I didn't think we needed a commission to validate the wrong that was done. In my opinion, we didn't need to get bogged down with time-consuming hearings, but instead, just go straight to the issue of redress for the damage done! I thought that every day we procrastinated, more of the aged *Issei* would die without ever experiencing the justice due them. My parents were among them.

However, I admit I changed my opinion on the commission hearings half way through the process. When

I attended some of the public hearings, I was amazed by how much participants were profoundly affected by publicly telling their stories to government officials. In addition, listening to each other's stories had great healing powers. One woman who had just finished her testimony physically shook for several minutes after her experience. What I found unforgettable was her comment after she finished. On her way out of the auditorium, she said to a few of us, "I feel like I had a piano, no, more like an elephant, on my back. Now it just melted away. " Then she added, "I never knew I could get such relief from telling my story. I can walk taller now."

The hearings were powerful, educational, therapeutic, and promoted community unity among the members of the audience. I began to understand how the hearings played a significant role in the redress effort. Over a six-month period, the CWRIC held public hearings in numerous American cities, including Seattle, providing a platform for more than 750 Japanese Americans and Alaska Natives to tell their stories and witness one another's stories.

In preparation for hearings in Seattle, the local chapter of the Japanese American Citizens League (JACL) was looking for people to give testimony. They particularly sought more *Issei* participation. Papa was 87 years old and living with me at the time. When I talked with Papa about the commission hearings, I was surprised that he was eager to testify. By this time, Papa was hard of hearing so I had a difficult time interviewing him in Japanese and then writing down his testimony in English.

As Papa recounted various episodes from his past, quite unexpectedly, he spoke of that day he boarded the train for a concentration camp. He said he heard his girls calling to him immediately after he got off the bus. Papa recalled walking slowly toward the fence where we were waiting. He thought perhaps he should ask permission from the guards to go to the fence, but he chose not to do so. He noted that "those menacing soldiers" were well armed with side arms as well as bayoneted rifles. Papa surmised it would be unlikely the soldiers would shoot him in front of the gathered crowd without at least a verbal warning, so he walked slowly toward his family behind the fence.

Papa told me he was surprised he made it all the way to the fence without being stopped. When a soldier ordered him to board the train that was the first time Papa questioned if he would ever see his family again.

On the day of the hearing, Papa was ready to share his story, pleased with the testimony we had prepared ahead of time. When it was Papa's turn, I helped him walk up the stairs to the stage and get seated, which was a challenge. Papa was quite deaf by this time so I had a signal for him to follow. "When I tap you on the shoulder three times, that means go ahead and introduce yourself and say a few things on your mind. Then I will take over and read your prepared testimony. Got it Papa?"

I put the microphone right up to his face and gave him the signal. Papa said in a loud voice in Japanese, *"Hajime yoo ka?"* ("Should I start now?") The audience got a big kick out of that. Then Papa quickly and proudly announced that he would soon be 88 years old. Only one of the nine commissioners was of Japanese descent, and aside from the audience, perhaps he was the only one who understood the significance of Papa turning 88. In Japanese culture, when people reach this age, they don a red vest and hat. Then they turn over all adult responsibilities to the next generation and begin their joyful second childhood.

Papa did a good job introducing himself and I was pleased I did not break down and sob while I read his testimony. I had heard that many others broke into sobs while testifying at the hearings. When I read the part where Papa, due to his increased deafness, had to give up listening to his favorite Japanese music, but could still hear his daughters calling to him at the train station four decades later, I feared I would cry. When I didn't cry, I was relieved, but my tears were yet to come. I did have to swallow my tears several times, but I thought I carried myself with dignity, too, along with Papa.

Papa's testimony was very touching. I wrote most of his testimony based on our interviews, and the effect of Papa introducing himself at the hearing put a whole new connection and power to his presentation. The spirit of the testimony was *all* Papa. The final conclusion of his story ended with two sentences.: "It takes a great country to admit its mistakes and make proper restitution. America has that greatness."

I heard many testimonies from Japanese Americans and read even more. Papa's testimony was not imbedded in any unusual circumstances, but it was my father's pain in his testimony that touched me so deeply. After the testimony, Papa got a well-deserved ovation. During the question and answer period, one of the nine commissioners, Judge William M. Marutani, (a judge with the Court of Common Pleas of Philadelphia) asked my father if the fishing company he worked for before the war was in Kodiak, Alaska." I was surprised by the question and wondered, *Where did Mr. Marutani get that information?*

Puzzled, I responded "Yes" on Papa's behalf. Then Mr. Marutani told Papa and the rest of the audience that during his college days, he worked for Papa in Kodiak to help pay for his college tuition. When the panel of elders had completed their testimonies, Judge Marutani left his seat and came all way to the lobby area to shake Papa's hand. Papa didn't remember him but was pleased to shake his hand. Here was the "boss" of the workers and the college student who had been looking for a job to pay tuition, facing one another four decades later. Now, the boss was an old man living frugally on his social security check and the young student became a revered court judge.

The speaker after my father was another elderly man who spoke of a daughter who had been suffering from a serious illness at the time his family was imprisoned at Minidoka. He told his story in Japanese and an interpreter relayed the story to the commission in English. I noticed the man shook as he told his story, but I wasn't sure if it was from nervousness, or anger, or recalling a sad occasion. His young daughter's illness was severe enough to cause her to be sent to a hospital outside the Minidoka camp. The hospital official sent word to the father that someone from the family needed to come to the hospital as soon as possible. This father had asked the camp administrator for permission to go to the hospital.

As his tragic story unfolded, I listened with bated breath. A groan rose up from my chest to my lips, thinking he would be denied permission. My tears began to flow as I witnessed his agony. Surprisingly, he told us that the camp administrator granted him permission to be with his daughter. However, the man then explained that because he was a prisoner, he had to be escorted by a security guard and he was told that he would be responsible to pay the per diem cost of the guard to accompany him. The man simply said, "I did not have the money. My daughter died alone among strangers."

I listened in stunned silence, afraid to miss one word, and yet unable to deal with what I was hearing. No longer could I hold back the tears. All the commissioners, with the exception of Judge Marutani, had no idea why I was crying because the man spoke in Japanese. They had to wait for the translation. In that moment, I wished I could've disappeared in a puff of smoke, far from the pain I felt as I listened to that man's story.

There were so many stories like my father's and the man who spoke after Papa. I had the privilege of hearing many stories from the Japanese American community. I attended every session in Seattle and was shaken to the core at the end of each day. These stories were filled with sorrow, pain, fear, but also with dignity, pride, courage, and compassion. I asked myself more than once, *How is it that people are able to retain hope when hope appears to have abandoned them? How is it that people can go through such devastating experiences and still demonstrate human kindness to their oppressors?*

After all the hearings and the findings were presented, the Commission concluded that the argument of "military necessity" was invalid as the major cause of the 1942 expulsion. There was no military necessity! Three major causes they identified were: (1) War Hysteria, (2) Race Prejudice, and (3) Failure of Political Leadership.

I often wondered why "greed" was not listed as one of the motivating causes. Many people profited financially as a benefit of the injustice perpetrated on the *Nikkei* people.

Papa died in December 1987, so his estate was ineligible to collect the redress award that was limited to people who were alive on the date President Ronald Reagan signed the Civil Liberties Act of 1988. This U.S. federal law granted reparations to Japanese Americans imprisoned during World War II. Payment for issuing the redress check went in the order of the age of the recipient. If Papa had lived for nine months more, I could have told him, "...the president of the United States of America, on behalf of all the people of the United States of America, sent a letter of apology to you Papa, along with this check for $20,000. Congratulations Papa!"

Mama received her redress check, but unfortunately, she had a stroke years prior to this event, so it was doubtful Mama understood the significance of the celebratory dinner her family and friends held for her. Justice was served, and for that, we were happy. Still, it was a shame that Mama could not know what the happy occasion was about. Wherever she is now, I'm sure Mama understands the whole picture.

Papa cannot be hurt anymore, but I still carry the pain and anguish Papa felt that day he was arrested and taken away from his family. It is through this pain that I can now better relate to the stories of other people in emotional turmoil today. It is Papa's pain that compels me to renew my resolve to share his dreams of justice and kindness with others. Papa's pain is a burden...but it is also a gift.

Mama and Papa before Mama's stroke, some twenty years before Papa testified before the commission.

PHOTO: NAKAGAWA PRIVATE COLLECTION

AFTERWORD

DÉJÀ VU

*"Those who cannot remember the past
are condemned to repeat it."*

—George Santayana
Philosopher, Poet & Writer

The first decade of the new millennium was not only a loud wake-up call for America; it was a huge "shake-up" call for me. After September 11, 2001, the widespread hysteria and fear toward anyone who looked Middle Eastern was appalling. Stories from the Muslim, Arab, and Sikh communities in the United States had a ring that was much too familiar. Children were called names at school, Middle Eastern-looking people were spit on, harassed, fired from jobs, and their property vandalized. They were beaten up and even murdered, and their homes and businesses vandalized. Our Japanese American stories from the 1940s, and the stories from the newly targeted communities were frighteningly similar; there was a feeling of *déjà vu.*

The media fanned people's fears and fueled hysteria. The U.S. government increased its power to intrude and detain people at the cost of civil liberties, and government groups targeted citizens based on their ethnicity. People began to perpetrate guilt by association on select groups. The accusers were usually those who understood little about a targeted group's history or culture. I kept thinking about the consistent and constant message from the Japanese American community to not let our country repeat the mistake of imprisoning a group of people based on ethnicity. A renewed sense of urgency inspired me to share my story of imprisonment and to express what American patriotism means to me, so I got off my comfortable duff to do my part. I wanted to make sure history doesn't repeat itself.

Initially, I began participating in a new group, Hate Free Zone (HFZ), formed after 9/11 in response to the hate crimes and discrimination targeting Muslims, Arab people, and many diverse communities of color. Under the dynamic leadership of the executive director, Pramila Jayapal, HFZ quickly became widely accepted as the key organization promoting services to the immigrant population. I was very impressed with Jayapal and HFZ's entire staff and volunteers and often agreed to participate in the organization's workshops and gatherings. At that time in my life, I was frequently involved in numerous high-profile public speaking engagements, sharing my story of imprisonment in Japanese American concentration camps.

When I first read the newspaper article about the Hamoui family, I felt personally connected to their story. In 2002, some fifteen FBI and Immigration and

Naturalization Service (INS) agents raided this Syrian family's home in Washington State. Safouh Hamoui, his wife, Hanan Ismail, and their daughter Nadin, a college student, had been arrested with guns pointed at their heads, and detained in Seattle for ten months. Three younger children in the family were removed from their home and relatives in the area cared for them.

At that time, the Hamoui family had been living in Washington since 1992, trying to get permanent asylum due to persecution in Syria. The family owned a local mom-and-pop grocery story and they were established members of their community. For an extended time, the family's legal status was unresolved and became a cause for immeasurable suffering. They were in prolonged legal limbo with the Department of Justice (DOJ) and the INS. The Hamouis were unsure if they would be allowed to stay in the U.S. or if they would be forced to return to Syria where they feared torture and possibly death.

When Mr. Hamoui's tourist visa expired, he had applied for asylum, fearful for his life if deported back to Syria. He received faulty legal support and subsequently, the INS denied his request for asylum. The similarities of the Hamoui family's experiences and my family's experiences were remarkably similar, even though they were sixty years apart. After the 9/11 crack down on hundreds of thousands of illegal immigrants, the FBI raided the Hamoui home. Exactly sixty years, plus one day, after the FBI invasion of our home in 1942, the Hamoui home was also similarly raided in 2002.

Takahashi Family (2-21-1942)	Hamoui Family (2-22-2002)
Family home raided	Family home raided
FBI agents	FBI agents
Early in the morning (still dark)	Early in the morning (still dark)
Month of February	Month of February
Swaggering intimidation by agents	Swaggering intimidation by agents
Guns were drawn	Guns were drawn
Family members frightened	Family members frightened
Father arrested	Father, Mother & Nadin arrested
Incarcerated at Seattle INS	Incarcerated at Seattle INS
Father loses his job	Father loses his business

In February 2003, Nadin Hamoui spoke at a public forum titled "Civil Liberties Denied: After December 7 and September 11." A crowd turned out with a sizable contingency of Japanese Americans. Nadin, who was barely 20 years old at the time, shared her story with maturity far beyond her years. She did not hide the anguish of her experience and spoke with honesty and courage. Many in the audience, including me, openly wept.

Then in June, HFZ held a public hearing in Washington, D.C., called "Justice for All." The HFZ invited me to share my experiences at their program. Nadin and I were scheduled to speak on the same day. We first met at dinner the night before our speaking engagements. Out of a dozen people at dinner, Nadin was the youngest and I was the oldest to participate in the program.

As Nadin and I shared our similar experiences of injustice at the hands of the U.S. government, we learned that both of our families were left devastated. Neither family knew what lay ahead for them. In the Hamoui family, Nadin and her parents were detained at the INS building in Seattle. Mr. Hamoui was separated from his wife and Nadin, and they were all held in isolation for ten months while the DOJ determined whether or not to deport the family. Their medical and dietary needs were ignored, and their health deteriorated. Astonished by Nadin's story, I also learned they were held at the same location where my father had been jailed for several months in 1942. I realized the INS building was essentially a prison and I was stunned that this building played a sad part in both our families.

Nadin did a superb job presenting her story, and although I had heard it before, I was glued to her every word. After our presentations, Nadin and I gave each other a big hug. I felt compelled to give Nadin an origami paper crane I had folded from a dollar bill. She was delighted and asked if I would teach her to fold the crane. Folding a crane out of paper money is not easy, but Nadin was a quick learner. She told me, "I can't wait to get home and teach my mother." Her radiant spirit and personality drew me closer to her.

Several months later, I attended a forum on immigrant justice in Seattle. My sister Kazu and Nadin's sister were on a panel to share their stories. Both sisters almost simultaneously recognized how similar their stories were and they both responded with great emotion. They hugged one other tightly as tears continued to stream down their faces. After that, I invited Nadin to serve on panels for our teacher training workshops. She did until the funding source dried up as a result of a tightened state budget.

In 2006, Mr. Hamoui and his family were finally granted asylum in the United States. The struggle took a tremendous toll on the family emotionally and financially, but justice was finally served. I was overjoyed to hear the news, but sad to learn the Hamoui family was left with depleted finances and debt. In the process, they lost their grocery store business. I thought of Mama and Papa having to start all over again after returning to Seattle after the war.

In 2008, HFZ changed its name to "One America, With Justice for All" and continues its good work on behalf of immigrants to the U.S. I was honored to have a small part in an excellent video the organization produced, "And Justice for All," which was spearheaded by Jayapal and HFZ. To this day, I am comforted to know there are so many good people who are willing to put forth their talents, skills, connections, and passions in order to support new Americans and the United States Constitution. This is patriotism in living color.

As the Author's Daughter

DeeAn S. Nakagawa

*E*ven though both of my parents were community and civil rights activists since the beginning of my life, I don't remember us siblings hearing much about the camp experience until we were adults or close to it. I'm quite certain my parents would say they talked to us about it but we didn't listen.

The first I remember hearing their stories was when I was in high school and the fight for Redress for Japanese Americans was starting. My maternal grandfather, who we called Papu, was living with us and I remember Mom working with him on his statement. He was such an optimist and even when remembering these difficult times, he would be so happy because of his love for his family. The story I remember most clearly was just after the war, Papu took his young daughter Mako to a Seattle diner. Mom excitedly asked if she could order a chicken pot pie. Papu checked to see if he had enough money and said yes. He was really pleased to see how much she enjoyed her special treat as he sipped his coffee. When they got home, Grandma fed a very hungry Papu. He only had enough money for Mom's pie and making her happy was a bigger priority for him. Thinking of this story makes me so proud of my Papu who sacrificed to make his daughter happy. I am also so very sad he had to make this sacrifice and profoundly angry because if not for the Japanese American imprisonment, my cannery foreman grandfather would have been easily able to afford chicken pot pie for the whole family.

Since Redress, Mom would speak about the incarceration experience at length both publicly and privately. In fact, my husband Eddie remembers the first words she ever spoke to him was answering the door and asking him his thoughts on American concentration camps for Japanese Americans. After many long conversations about the Power of Words and Japanese American incarceration, Mom was disappointed when we (family) became disinterested or changed the subject.

Mom has been diligently working on improving and editing her stories for many years. When I read the manuscript before publication, I was really pleased with how touching her stories are. I had a very difficult time reading her stories for so many reasons including feeling sad for what my grandparents suffered and, to be blunt, pissed off that they were made to suffer.

I took the opportunity in writing this statement for Mom's book to learn from *Sansei* family and friends about their experiences having incarcerated parents. While some had heard about the camps for the entirety of their lives, most heard almost nothing unless something came up incidentally. For example, one friend said that when she went to the Puyallup Fair with her family, her dad would talk about how he lived in the horse stalls there but otherwise, he didn't talk about his experience being imprisoned.

Most of us *Sansei* agree that many of the older generation were too ashamed, too embarrassed, too angry or the memories were too painful to talk about. Even when the reparation payments were being distributed, some open discussions seemed to be more about what to do with the money rather than what was lost and what the real costs of the incarcerations were for those who were imprisoned.

Mom wrote a charming and, unfortunately, currently relevant memoir from a child's perspective. Uncle Yogi's illustrations perfectly capture the *kimochi* (feeling) of her stories. I'm honored to be able to round out this family project and hope it will be educational, emotional and potentially evocative for readers.

ACKNOWLEDGMENTS

*M*any people helped me bring this book to publication and I am very much indebted to all of them. First and foremost is the gratitude I have for my mother and father. They are referred to as "Mama" and "Papa" in the stories, but their proper names are Hisako Takahashi and Masao Takahashi. They provided me with as normal a childhood as possible in abnormal circumstances, so much so, that I thought my childhood was normal. There is no doubt that each of them paid a high price in their efforts to protect their children while coping with their own miseries at the time.

I want to acknowledge and thank my sisters, Kazzie Katayama, Nobie Takahashi, and Midori Akagi. They not only shared memories of those "camp days" with me, they described many of their own rich experiences that I could write about.

Each of my three children, in their own way, gave me emotional support that spurred me on to do my best. For me, writing is not a pleasurable activity. I needed the closeness of my children to urge me on. So thank you to Daren, Kenji, and DeeAn Nakagawa. DeeAn and my son-in-law, Eddie Cukierman, shepherded the project by finding and scanning photos, making sure the computer was working, sending the manuscript to my publisher, and countless other tasks that required their talents and skills. DeeAn worked closely on the final details with my publisher to the very end.

The person who made these stories come alive is my brother-in-law, Mits Katayama. I have always admired his talent as an artist, but I think he outdid himself with his illustrations for my stories. He caught the *kimochi* —the heart, the essence, the core spirit—of each of the stories. I jokingly complained to him that his drawings were even better than my stories. He was a modest man, but he did not disagree with me. Mits died before this book was completed, but he knew it would see the light of day. It's always hard to lose someone, especially someone so special.

My close friends Kayko Watanabe, May Namba, and Barbara Johnstone gave me crucial early feedback on my stories from which I profited greatly. Kayko had been a child prisoner as well and she contributed her important perspective. May, who was a young woman at the time of the incarceration, read the stories with particular attention to camp details. Barbara gave me the perspective of a *hakujin,* a white person, who didn't experience camp life, but had great interest in my stories and always gave me her blatantly honest reaction. Each one gave me honest critical comments as well as persistent encouragement to write.

It was most convenient to have two of my neighbors contribute so much to putting my stories on paper. Kathy Sugiyama used her skills as an editor to help smooth out the rough edges of my writing, and Mary Granger spent many hours patiently helping me overcome my frustrations with the computer.

Historical scholars Tetsuden Kashima, Ph.D. and David Yamaguchi, Ph.D. were both instrumental in moving my daydream of producing a book into the realm of possibility. Their support and professional advice were of particular help, in addition to their sensitivities to hear the cries and feel the anger. They care.

I asked the writer David Takami to give me his quick reaction to my draft stories. He went far beyond the simple reaction I had asked for. His painstaking corrections and suggestions gave me confidence that my stories were worth publication because he was so willing to invest so much of his time and talent.

Cherry Kinoshita was invaluable as a tireless advocate for redress and a committed community organizer. She had such a vivid memory, a perceptive ear for facts and tones, and a quick eye for errors. I greatly appreciated her helpful feedback.

Karen Yoshitomi was a great partner in workshop presentations about the incarceration of Japanese Americans. She was a valuable asset and support in filling in my blanks in the area of technology and research. Organized and thoughtful, she was serious when she needed to be, in addition to having a wicked sense of humor. Karen is a gem.

Nancy Rawles used her skills as a published author to work with me on the final edit. She was not afraid to roll up her sleeves and go through the manuscript line by line with me. I enjoyed her company and at times I had to work doubly hard to get through the final edits. Because of her dedication, I can now call myself an author.

Finally, I am grateful to Maureen R. Michelson, publisher of NewSage Press, for bringing this project to fruition and guiding me to transform my children's stories into a full-fledged memoir. We began working together in 2013 to develop my manuscript. Her work as an editor has been amazing. She helped me understand the importance of my story and its contribution to the body of literature on the imprisonment of Japanese Americans. I didn't know a book needed to be designed, so I was enthralled by the artistry of NewSage Press's book designer Sherry Wachter. Magic happened. I am grateful for Sherry's attention to design details and the presentation of Mits's illustrations.

So many people listened to me read my stories and helped by making comments. I cannot possibly recognize them all. If I tried to name them individually, I would surely leave some names out. To all those people, please know that I very much appreciate your active listening, your sensitive reactions, and your belief in me as a writer. To thank you all would take another book.

Mostly, I am grateful for the opportunity to tell my story, and for my parents whose shoulders I stand on. To them, and to all the giants who carried their children on their shoulders and let us see over the fences, I am *arigatai* —thankful.

Okagesama de—with recognition and gratitude for your part in my life.

ABOVE:
Mako on her 80th birthday in 2017 with her grown children, from left to right; son-in-law Eddie, daughter DeeAn, son Kenji (Bradly), and son Daren.

LEFT:
Mako and her sisters at her niece's wedding. From right, Mako, Midori, Kazu, and Nobu.

ILLUSTRATION: MITS KATAYAMA

Takahashi · Family · Tree
Christmas · 2013

ABOUT THE AUTHOR

*M*ako Nakagawa celebrated her 81st birthday in February 2018 and completed her memoir, *Child Prisoner in American Concentration Camps,* which she had been working on for more than a decade. This book is based on her original manuscript of stories for young readers, *Camp Child,* self-published in 2007. Her brother-in-law, Mits Katayama, a well-established commercial artist, created original illustrations to accompany Mako's stories.

Mako began her formal education at five years old as a child prisoner in American concentration camps built to confine people of Japanese ancestry living on the West Coast during World War II. In her adult years, Mako became an educator, earning her M.A. in Education from Seattle University. She specialized in multicultural education and was the Program Director for Seattle Public School's Ethnic Cultural Heritage Program (RAINBOW). In 1976, she oversaw development of a RAINBOW curriculum for a national market and received a Washington Education Association Curriculum Award in 1977 for her work on this project.

Mako served as principal at two Seattle elementary schools in the 1970s and 1980s. She went on to become Program Administrator for Multicultural Education, Basic Skills and the Curriculum unit of the Washington State Office of the Superintendent of Public Instruction (OSPI).

Her growing concern for Japanese American civil rights and redress matched her ongoing concern for multicultural education. In 1991, Mako started her own business, Mako & Associates, providing contract diversity training programs. As an accomplished public speaker and writer, Mako emphasized the "power of words" and the importance of describing the imprisonment of Japanese Americans with accurate terminology—not with euphemisms that mislead and distort the truth.

Mako was an active member of the Japanese American Citizens League (JACL) and other groups to create policies and plans to educate the general public about the injustices in recent U.S. history, in particular, the imprisonment of 120,000 people of Japanese ancestry living on the West Coast.

Over the years she has made numerous presentations on her experiences as a child prisoner and conducted a series of workshops on the subject for teachers, organizations, and students from elementary through college. Mako has been the recipient of numerous awards and honors for her work as an educator, including from the national Committee on School Desegregation, the Asian Education Advisory Council, and the Japanese American Citizens League.

Mako lives in Seattle and has three adult children. She enjoys Seattle sports including the Seahawks, Sounders, and Mariners, and spending time with her family and friends. This is her first published book and if you ask her—her last!

ABOUT THE ILLUSTRATOR

*M*its Katayama was a well-
established and talented artist
of renown in his profession as
a commercial artist. While the
recipient of numerous awards
and recognitions, they were not
his motivation. He was recognized by the Seattle Professional
Graphic Artists Guild almost
annually but his wife says she

only knew he was being honored because she was invited
to attend. Mits illustrated a number of children's books
for Parenting Press, including *What About Me?*, *12 Ways
to Get Your Parents' Attention (Without Hitting Your Sister)*
and *Feelings for Little Children* series, among others.

Mits began drawing as a boy and spent most of his
adult life drawing and painting primarily as a commercial artist. He credited his *Issei* (first-generation) parents,
along with a teacher in his small three-room rural school,
for encouraging him as an artist early along.

Mits was incarcerated at Minidoka concentration
camp in 1942 as a young teen and spent three years

there with his family. At this time, he was living with his widowed mother and younger brother in a small rural area south of Seattle. Mits had many distinct memories from what he called his "camp days" that he drew from in his detailed illustrations for this book. During his imprisonment, Mits became well-known in the community for his singing. His crooning style earned him the title of the "Japanese Frank Sinatra." His public appearances were in stark contrast to his shy personality, but he sang at many weddings, festivals, bazaars, and family gatherings.

After the war, Mits returned to Seattle and graduated from Garfield High School and later, the Edison Technical School, now called Seattle Central Community College. He served in the U.S. Signal Corps as a radio operator—and as an artist assigned to paint names on Army helmets.

Mits married Kazu Takahashi (Mako's eldest sister) in Seattle on September 20, 1953. They both had many names. Kazu is Kazzie to friends and Kai to family. Francis Mitsuru was Mits to friends and Yogi to family, inspired by his drawings of Yogi Bear. To both, the names most important have always been Hamma (Grandma) and Bumpa (Grandpa) to Sara. Mits and Kazzie raised their three sons—Mark, Glenn and Stevan—in Seattle.

Mits loved to play golf and tennis, to shoot pool, and to watch the Seahawks and Mariners. Mits passed away in November 2014, but his spirit lives on through his art.

CPSIA information can be obtained
at www.ICGtesting.com
Printed in the USA
LVHW082039120319
610186LV00002B/1/P